Contents

TRANSPORT AND ROAD RESEARCH LABORATORY
Department of Transport

ORCED CONCRETE

LONDON: HMSO

ISBN 0 11 550979 8

The views expressed in this review are not necessarily those of the Department of Transport

HMSO publications are available from:

HMSO Publications Centre
(Mail and telephone orders only)
PO Box 276, London, SW8 5DT
Telephone orders 071-873 9090
General enquiries 071-873 0011
(queuing system in operation for both numbers)

HMSO Bookshops
49 High Holborn, London, WC1V 6HB   071-873 0011 (counter service only)
258 Broad Street, Birmingham, B1 2HE   021-643 3740
Southey House, 33 Wine Street, Bristol, BS1 2BQ   (0272) 264306
9-21 Princess Street, Manchester, M60 8AS   061-834 7201
80 Chichester Street, Belfast, BT1 4JY   (0232) 238451
71 Lothian Road, Edinburgh, EH3 9AZ   031-228 4181

HMSO's Accredited Agents
(see Yellow Pages)

and through good booksellers

Glossary

a	crack depth of surface flaw or half-width of penetration flaw (mm)
a_v	shear span, the distance between the line of action of a load and the critical shear section (mm)
A	crack area (mm²)
A_{sv}	cross sectional area of stirrup (mm²)
A_p	cross sectional area of prestressing steel (mm²)
A_s	cross sectional area of reinforcing steel (mm²)
α_e	modular ratio, E_s/E_c
α_p	Poisson's ratio
b	the width of a concrete beam
d	the effective depth of a concrete beam
$\varnothing$	bar diameter (mm)
D	bend (mandrel) diameter (mm)
D_c	compressive force (N)
δ	separation distance (mm)
e_i	error component of a data point
E	Modulus of elasticity (N/mm²)
E_c	Modulus of elasticity for concrete (N/mm²)
E_s	Modulus of elasticity for steel (N/mm²)
ε	strain (μ,microstrain)
ε_{max}	total maximum cycle strain
ε_e	recovered cyclic strain
ε_t	time dependent strain
ε'_{cyc}	rate of change of strain per cycle
f	static ultimate strength (N/mm²)
f_p	static ultimate tensile strength of prestressing steel (N/mm²)
f_y	yield stress of hot rolled steel (N/mm²)
$f_{0.2}$	0.2 per cent proof stress of cold worked steel (N/mm²)
F	frequency, cycles per second (Hz)
G	strain energy release rate (J/sec) in linear fracture mechanics
γ	partial safety factor
H	wave height (m)
J	rate of force separation (J/sec) in non-linear fracture mechanics
K	stress intensity factor
L	base length of the portion of the point load influence line which contains the greatest ordinate
m	stress exponent in S-N relationship $(\sigma_r)^m N = \text{constant}$
M	bending moment (Nm)
n	number of cycles
N	number of cycles to failure, endurance
N_p	number of cycles of preloading
P	probability

Q   shear force (N)

R $\sigma_{min}/\sigma_{max}$ stress ratio

s_v stirrup spacing (mm)

S σ_r stress range (N/mm^2) also 2S is area under force separation curve

S-N curve, the characteristic relationship between stress range and endurance for a material (eg concrete, steel), component (eg Class R1 corroded reinforcing bar) or design feature (eg Class D welding detail)

σ_r range of a repeated stress cycle, the algebraic sum of σ_{max} and σ_{min} (N/mm^2)

σ_{max} maximum stress (N/mm^2)

σ_{min} minimum stress (N/mm^2)

σ_{rm} mean level of a repeated stress cycle (N/mm^2)

σ_{ro} stress range for zero mean stress, $\sigma_{max} = +\sigma_r/2$ and $\sigma_{min} = -\sigma_r/2$ (N/mm^2)

σ_s stress in main reinforcing steel (N/mm^2)

σ_{sv} stress in stirrups (N/mm^2)

σ_p stress in prestressing steel (N/mm^2)

t_f time to fatigue failure (seconds)

T   period time (second) of a stress cycle

U_M mechanical energy (J)

V   shear force (N) due to ultimate load

V_{sv} ultimate shear force carried by stirrups

ω Palmgren-Miner failure criterion

x   depth to neutral axis of concrete beam (mm)

z   lever arm of concrete beam (mm)

Z   tensile force (N)

SUBSCRIPTS

c   concrete, compression

cyc   cycle, cyclic

e   elastic

i   general data point

f   fatigue

k   characteristic

m   mean

max   maximum

min   minimum

M   material, mechanical

p   prestressing steel

P   preloading, Poisson

r   range

s   reinforcing steel

spl   splitting

t   tension, time

u   ultimate

v   shear

y   yield

Abstract

Generally, fatigue has not been considered to be a problem in the design of reinforced concrete structures. Until the 1960s, reinforcement was mild steel and the stresses permitted in the steel and the concrete were such that fatigue failure was believed to be impossible. Over the years, higher working stresses were permitted and, in particular, high yield reinforcing bars were introduced. Design rules were issued to control cracking and prohibit the welding of reinforcement unless the risk of fatigue was negligible. In response to the need for guidance on the subject, the Transport and Road Research Laboratory carried out a coordinated programme of fatigue testing, including work on the fatigue performance of reinforced and prestressed concrete beams. In recent years, international collaboration through the Comité Euro-International du Béton (CEB) produced case studies showing that fatigue can occur in reinforced concrete structures in combination with other causes of deterioration. A great deal of research has been carried out, leading to a better understanding of the fatigue behaviour of plain concrete, the various types of reinforcing bars in air, in concrete, continuous, welded, lapped or coupled and the effect of corrosion. Research on reinforced beams and slabs included tests on permanent formwork and the study of prestressed beams of normal and lightweight concrete. The work of TRRL and many others is reviewed and finally a summary is given of current design rules, mainly as formulated in the CEB-FIP Model Code, with recommendations for assessing the fatigue life of new structures and structures in service.

1 Introduction

1.1 Early research on fatigue

Although it was already known that metals fracture under frequently repeated stresses lower than their ultimate static strength - Fairbairn (1864) published research on fatigue - it was the extensive work of Wohler (1871) on ferrous metals using laterally loaded rotating shafts that established two important results:

1. Fatigue strength depends on the range, σ_r, of fluctuating stress, where σ_r is the algebraic difference between the extreme stresses, σ_{max} and σ_{min}, rather than the level of σ_{max}.

2. Reversed stresses, even well within the elastic limit, repeated many times can cause fracture.

It was found that lower levels of fluctuating stress required a greater number of cycles, N, to cause failure and appeared that there was a stress range, known as the fatigue limit which could be applied an unlimited number of times without causing failure. Fatigue is characterised by the initiation of a crack which propagates until sudden failure occurs. The fracture surfaces are crystalline with no sign of yield even in the case of ductile steel. The relationship between fatigue limit and stress level was delineated by Professor J Goodman in diagrams such as Figure 1.1, in which the allowable stress range or fatigue limit, σ_r, is the shaded area between σ_{max} and σ_{min}. It is convenient to express all stresses as proportions of the ultimate static strength, f.

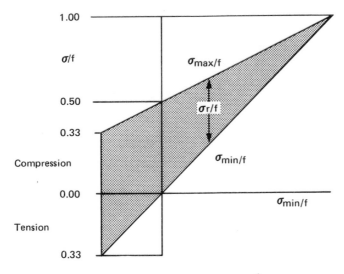

Fig. 1.1
Goodman Diagram

1

Morley (1940) pointed out that any stress cycle can be regarded as a constant mean stress, σ_m, and a reversed stress cycle + and - $0.5\sigma_r$ and gave two equations to define limits of σ_r which are typical of many metals for various values of *tensile* σ_m:

$$\sigma_r = \sigma_{ro}(1 - (\sigma_m/f)^2) \text{ due to Gerber (1874)}$$

$$\sigma_r = \sigma_{ro}(1 - \sigma_m/f) \text{ a modified form of Goodman}$$

where σ_{ro} is the value of σ_r for $\sigma_{rm} = 0$, that is stress reversal, and f is the static ultimate strength.

Limited test data on the fatigue performance of mild steel supported Gerber's parabola but the modified Goodman straight line had the merit of being both simple and on the safe side.

Given sufficient experimental results, modified Goodman diagrams can be constructed by plotting σ_{max} versus σ_{min} for various endurances as Figure 2.12.

Sir J A Ewing (1899) experimenting with long wires found strain lag in repeated loading and unloading cycles and the accumulation of local strain (hysteresis) suggested an explanation of fatigue behaviour. Fatigue is characterised by the initiation of a crack which propagates until sudden failure occurs. The fracture surfaces are crystalline with no sign of yield even for a ductile steel.

J H Smith (1910) described the effect of higher carbon content on the mechanical properties of steel, notably the loss of ductility with the increase in ultimate strength. Smith diagrams show stress range, σ_r, versus mean stress, σ_m, for a stated endurance, N, commonly 2 million cycles and a stated maximum stress, σ_{max}, such as $0.55f_u$.

However the basic fatigue characteristic of a material, a graph showing the stress range, σ_r, as ordinate against N, the number of cycles to failure, known as an S-N curve, is usually presented with σ_r against log N as in Figure 3.1 or log σ_r against log N as in Figure 3.3. An S-N curve is derived from numerous fatigue tests, results of which are notorious for scatter, as a "best fit" providing a prescribed confidence level. For some steels a fatigue limit may be apparent after 1 million cycles whilst for others there is no convincing flattening of the S-N curve after 100 million cycles.

S-N curves can also be produced for concrete but there is no fatigue limit since high cycle low stress loading can contribute to fatigue damage.

Information on the statistical treatment of test results and the calculation of confidence levels is given in Appendix 1.

1.2 Assessing fatigue life

Nowadays there are two approaches to the assessment of fatigue life:

1   Fracture mechanics - considering local stress intensity initiating a crack which is propagated by the energy derived from further loading cycles

2   S-N/Palmgren-Miner - estimating cumulative damage due to appropiate load spectra to achieve acceptable probability that fatigue failure will not occur before a given number of cycles.

An outline of the fracture mechanics approach will be found in Appendix 2.

The second, the classical approach, is still the more popular and is adopted in various codes. The cumulative damage concept was enunciated by Palmgren (1924) in a paper on the life of ball bearings and was developed independently by Miner (1945) using the results of fatigue tests on high strength aluminium alloy specimens.

To check the fatigue life of a structural element the first requirement is to identify critical sections of the element and the spectrum of all its service loading cycles with the frequency and the maximum and minimum stresses of each block of loading. If there is structural interaction, as with wind or wave loading, it may be appropriate to use a deterministic procedure; see 6.2. and Appendix 3. Details of the standard fatigue loading vehicles and traffic flows to be used for highway and railway bridge design are given in BS 5400: Part 10. Taking the appropriate S-N curve, the endurance, N, is then found for the stress range of each loading cycle. The fatigue damage due to each block of the loading spectrum is n/N where n is the number of occurrences of that block during the fatigue life considered. The criterion to be satisfied is that the Palmgren-Miner summation for all cycles, $\Sigma n/N \leq 1$ normally but see Appendix 4.

A new structure can thus be designed for an specified notional life.

Assessing the residual fatigue life of an existing structure involves estimating the fatigue loading and damage it has already sustained.

Early reinforced concrete structures relied on the use of mild steel reinforcement at maximum design stresses well below its so called fatigue limit, at least 70 per cent of its ultimate tensile strength. In the 1960s high yield deformed bars were introduced together with higher design stresses closer to 50 per cent of the ultimate static strength of the material such that fatigue could become a problem during the life of a structure.

In the absence of comprehensive data on the fatigue strength of reinforcing bars made in the United Kingdom, Menzies (1971) used test data from the United States, Germany, Austria and Japan to produce modified Goodman diagrams which related fatigue strength to endurances.

Bannister (1969) conducted constant amplitude tests on 22 concrete beams reinforced with hot rolled deformed high yield bars of United Kingdom manufacture and showed that Menzies' modified Goodman diagrams were conservative. Most of the test data was for stress ratios, $R = \sigma_{min}/\sigma_{max}$, between zero and 0.3 and fatigue lives between 100,000 and 2 million although some of Bannister's work extended to endurances of 10 million cycles.

This provided interim information to update design rules but it was necessary to extrapolate the modified Goodman diagrams to take account of longer and shorter endurances. Considering typical structural members under highway bridge loading in critical combinations with other loading such as temperature effects, the Department of Transport (1973) found that fatigue life would be acceptable if design stress range was limited to 325 N/mm² for cold worked or hot rolled high yield bars in highway structures. This avoided the need to carry out fatigue checks in reinforced concrete design. The Department also prohibited the welding of any reinforcement except in members where the fatigue risk was negligible.

There was a need for data on endurances of more than 100 million cycles and the present State-of-the-Art review outlines work carried out at the Transport and Road Research Laboratory and elsewhere in response to this need.

1.3   Growth in the use of reinforced concrete

Since the introduction of reinforced concrete to the United Kingdom at the beginning of the century there has been an enormous increase in this form of construction. Reinforced concrete is now commonplace in industrial, commercial and public buildings and structures, railways, roads and bridges. In particular there has been an upsurge since the 1950s in the construction of new towns and cities, urban reconstruction and the construction of new roads and motorways. For example the growth in numbers of trunk road and motorway bridges is shown in Figure 1.2

A census of all highway bridges undertaken in 1987 under the auspices of the Department of Transport indicated the total numbers and estimated numbers of substandard bridges given in Table 1.1.

Although much of the research reviewed here is concerned with concrete bridges, the principles and data can be applied to any reinforced concrete structure which carries repeated loading cycles.

Figure 1.3 shows how the strength of 1:2:4 concrete and corresponding design stresses for concrete and reinforcing steel have increased since the 1920s.

Reinforced concrete started to have an impact on the construction scene after the First World War but its real heyday has been post-1945. It has been estimated that 60 per cent of all cement in the United Kingdom was produced and used since 1960.

4

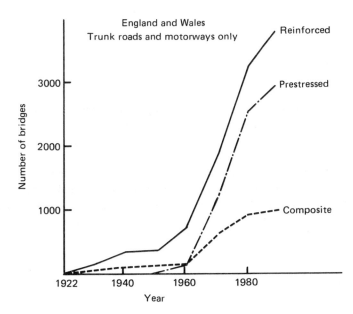

Fig. 1.2
*Numbers of concrete highway bridges
(Bridges Engineering Division, Department of Transport)*

TABLE 1.1

Numbers of highway bridges in the United Kingdom

	Totals	*Estimated numbers substandard*
Masonry	34,901	2,800
Concrete	10,372	3,330
Metal	7,909	5,120

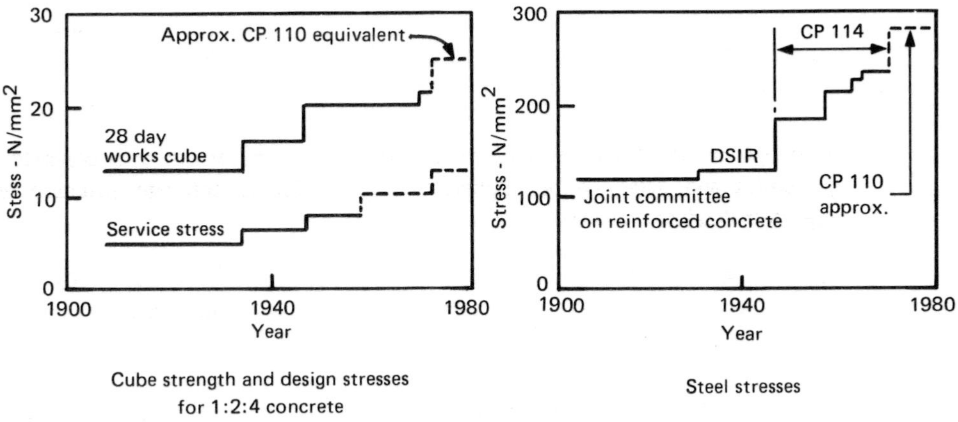

Cube strength and design stresses
for 1:2:4 concrete

Steel stresses

Fig. 1.3
*Cube strength of 124 concrete and design stresses since the 1920s
(Beeby, 1986, British Cement Association)*

1.4 Case studies

RILEM Committees 36-RDL (1984) and 65-MDB (1986) have found that fatigue can occur in a concrete structure if excessive cracking and deflection develop under repeated loading. CEB General Task Group 15 reported comprehensively on the subject (1988) giving details of 17 case histories of structural unserviceability in which fatigue was a contributing factor. The 17 case histories are grouped below to identify the associated factors.

1.4.1 Plain concrete

5	Bridge deck expansion joints disrupted after 3 to 10 years.	Sweden Serkitjis (1981)	Ingress of deicing salt.
9	Motorway pavement cracked in most heavily loaded lanes.	Holland Leewis (1986)	Several other factors unnamed.
13	Factory floor found unfit for installation of knee hinge presses	Sweden Serkitjis (1981)	Vibration and 95 Db caused by test running were unacceptable for working environment and caused cracking.
14	Footing for paper pulp cutting knife hit with great force at 1.7 Hz cracked after 6 years	Sweden Serkitjis (1981)	Resonance.

1.4.2 Reinforced concrete

1	Cantilevered bridge deck after about 10 years	United States Forsyth & Stahl (1983)	Secondary tensile stresses due to repeated deflection of cantilever support beam, insufficient distribution reinforcement, corrosion due to deicing salt, wear of concrete running surface.
2	Numerous bridge decks after a few years	Japan Sonada *et al* (1982) Matsui *et al* (1986)	Repeated shear and repeated torsional effects.

4	30 bridge decks after 25 to 50 years depending on intensity of traffic	Holland Eggermont (1986)	No factors other than fatigue of the concrete under wheel tracks.
6	Continuous main beams of bridge built 1943	Sweden Serkitjis (1981)	220 tonnes transformer almost caused collapse in 1950s; timber trucks exceed 51tonnes design load. Insufficient shear steel.
7	Travelling crane track support structure. Holding down bolts and column heads failed after about 2 years	Sweden ditto	Insufficient reinforcement.
8	Viaduct deck slab after about 50 years	Sweden ditto	Carbonation of concrete
10	Factory floor slab. In situ topping failed	United Kingdom Hughes & Dundar (1968)	Excessive cracking and deflection led to isolation of precast planks
15	Woodchip processor built in 1967 recracked in 1971 despite repairs	Sweden Serkitjis (1981)	Complex loading and vibration from hydraulic machinery, tractors and pressure of woodchips.
16	Paper mill built in the late 1930s	Finland Serkitjis (1981)	Low concrete strength. Long term loading and vibration. Oil penetration.
17	Pile driving. 6% of concrete piles are damaged during driving.	Sweden Serkitjis (1981)	Crushing of pile head. Transverse cracks caused by tension waves and longitudinal cracks follow the line of the reinforcement.

1.4.3 Prestressing steel

| 3 | Curved prestressed bridge developed 2mm cracks at joints. Tendons failed by brittle fracture at rolled thread near sleeves. | Germany Ruhrberg & Schaumann (1982) | Traffic induced stresses in uncracked concrete 16 N/mm^2, in cracked concrete 198 N/mm^2 Fatigue strength of sleeved connection 70 N/mm^2 for 2 million cycles. |

11	Of 17 prestressed concrete bridges demolished after 20 to 30 years, 3 found to have tendons with a slight loss of fatigue strength.	Germany Konig & Sturm (1986)	Corrosion in partially grouted ducts with pitting commonly 20 to 30 microns and 500 microns as the exception. Pits of 150 to 250 microns can reduce fatigue strength as much as 50%.
12	Congress Hall, Berlin Collapse of south arch 20 May 1980 due to tendon failure.	Germany Stiglat, Linder & Peters (1980)	Ingress of water to open cracks Carbonation and chloride attack of joint concrete. Hydrogen induction at corrosion pits.

CEB Bulletin No.188 (1988) concludes that fatigue is unlikely to be the sole cause of deterioration and lists the following others:

1   Repeated deflections leading to secondary stresses.

2   Increased live load intensity and frequency.

3   Live load stresses much greater than dead load stresses.

4   Repeated impact and other forces.

5   Vibration, particularly when associated with contaminants

6   Unconfined or poorly confined points of application of repeated loads.

7   Fretting, pitting and chemical attack, especially in prestressed concrete.

8   Carbonation, especially in reinforced concrete.

1.5   Inspection and assessment

Price et al. (1982) noted that the following design and construction features need special attention if fatigue is to be avoided:

1   Grouting of prestressing ducts

2   Anchorages and other zones of stress concentration.

3   Structural connections, lapping, splicing and welding of reinforcement.

The principal structural effects of fatigue appear to be:

1   Excessive cracking, corrosion and corrosion fatigue.

2   Excessive deformation and loss of prestress.

3   Reduced stiffness and increased liveliness.

The above features and effects deserve careful attention during inspections.The basic approach to the assessment of fatigue damage in reinforced concrete is by close inspection of "hot spots" for cracking or crushing of concrete, possibly using the following specialist techniques (See Figure 2.3) in certain cases:

1   Ultrasonic equipment may detect cracks

2   Accoustic emission from cracks may be detected as they develop

3   Vibration monitoring may detect changes in stiffness.

Two developments enliven interest in the problem of fatigue:

1   The need to assess the remaining life of damaged structures

2   The availability of well based assessment rules

1.6 Summary

Fatigue strength depends upon the range of cyclic stress - the lower the stress, the greater the number of cycles to failure. For ferrous metals it was assumed that there is a stress, known as the fatigue limit, that can be repeated indefinitely.

Fatigue characteristics can be presented in Goodman diagrams and S-N curves.

Fatigue life can be assessed by fracture mechanics or more commonly by the classical Palmgren-Miner cumulative damage criterion $\Sigma n/N \leq 1$.

Little of the early work went beyond 2 million cycles but data are now available for low stress ranges up to more than 100 million cycles which contribute to fatigue damage.

CEB General Task Group 15 collated 17 case histories of structural failure in which fatigue was a contributing (but not prime) factor. Certain design and construction features need attention to minimise the risk of fatigue in new structures. Engineering inspections of structures in service should include special attention to fatigue prone sites.

1.7 References

BANNISTER, J L (1969) The behaviour of reinforcing bars under fluctuating stress. Concrete, October 1969.

BEEBY, A W and HAWES, F L (1986) Action and reaction in concrete design, 1935-1985. CCA Reprint 3/86. British Cement Association.

CEB (1988) Fatigue of concrete structures. State-of-the-Art Report. Bulletin d'Information No.188.

DEPARTMENT OF TRANSPORT, (1973) Reinforced concrete for highway structures. Technical Memorandum BE1/73

DEPARTMENT OF TRANSPORT, (1987) The assessment of highway bridges and structures. Bridge census and sample survey

EGGERMONT, P (1986) Case Study: Concrete bridge decks. Bridge Building Department of the Ministry of Verkeer en Waterstaat, Voorburg, The Netherlands. Unpublished.

EWING, Sir J A (1899) British Association Report, p.502.

FAIRBAIRN (1864) Philosophical Transactions of the Royal Society.

FORSYTH, B and STAHL, F L (1983) Throgs Neck Bridge: Why did its deck deteriorate? Civil Engineering, ASCE, pp 50-52, July 1983.

GERBER (1874) Relation between superior and inferior stresses of a cycle of limiting stress. Zeit. Bayerischen Arch. Ing.-Vereins.

HUGHES, B P and DUNDAR, C (1968) Fatigue and the ability of composite precast and in situ concrete slabs to distribute concentrated loads. The Structural Engineer, Vol. 64B, no 1, March 1968.

KÖNIG, G and STURM, R (1986) Analysis of reports about demolition work of prestressed construction, concerning the long term behaviour of prestressing steel. Technische Hochschule, Darmstadt. Unpublished.

LEEWIS, M (1986) Case Studies: Concrete pavements. Dutch Cement and Concrete Association, 's-Hertogenbosch, The Netherlands. Unpublished.

MATSUI, S, SONADA, K, OKAMURA, H and OKADA, K (1986) Concepts for deterioration of highway bridge decks and fatigue studies. International Symposium. Fundamental theory of reinforced and prestressed concrete. NIT Nanjing, China, September 18-20 1986

MENZIES, J B (1971) The fatigue strength of steel reinforcement in concrete. Building Research Station Current Paper CP16/71.

MINER, M A (1945) Cumulative damage in fatigue. American Society of Mechanical Engineers. Transactions, vol. 67 pp A159-A164.

MORLEY, A (1940) Strength of materials. Ninth edition.

PALMGREN, A (1924) Die Lebensdauer von Kugellagern. Zeitschrift des Vereines deutscher Ingenieren. Band 68, Nr. 14, pp339-341.

PRICE, W I J, TRICKLEBANK, A K and HAMBLY, E C (1982) Fatigue considerations in the design of concrete offshore structures. IABSE Colloquium. Fatigue of steel and concrete structures, Lausanne.

RILEM (1984) Long term random loading of concrete structures. Report by Committee 36-RDL.

RILEM (1986) Dynamic behaviour of concrete structures. Report by Committee 65-MDB.

RUHRBERG, R and SCHAUMANN (1982) Case 13303, pp130-137, Schaden anBrucken und anderen Ingenieurbauwerken Ursachen und Erkenntnisse. Oct.

SERKITJIS, M (1981) An inventory of damage to structures in the Nordic countries. Division of Building Technology, Chalmers University of Technology, Gothenburg.

SMITH, J H (1910) Journal Iron and Steel Inst. No 11, pp256-257.

SPOONER, D C (1986) Materials - the recipe for successful concrete, 1935-1985. CCA Reprint 1/86. British Cement Association.

SONADA, K and HORIKAMA, T (1982) Fatigue strength of concrete slabs under moving loads. Colloquium. Fatigue of steel and concrete structures, IABSE Reports Vol. 37, pp 456-462.

STIGLAT, K, LINDER, R and PETERS, H (1980) Partial collapse of the Congress Hall, Berlin - Causes of damage. Comprehensive report.Beton- und Stahlbetonbau, Vol.12 pp 281-294. (in German)

WOHLER (1871) Engineering. Vol. xi.

2 Plain concrete

2.1 Background

Raithby and Whiffen(1968) of the Road Research Laboratory reviewed early research on fatigue of concrete. The first fatigue curve for concrete cubes in compression, shown in Figure 2.1, was published by Van Ornum (1903).

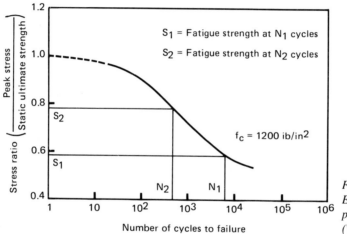

Fig. 2.1
Endurance curve for concrete prisms
(Van Ornum, 1903)

Van Ornum found no endurance limit for concrete similar to that which had been assumed for steel but he concluded that concrete had a fatigue strength about 55 per cent of its static ultimate strength for a life of 7000 cycles. Subsequently others found the same percentage for endurances up to about 10 million cycles. Van Ornum observed the changing shape of the stress-strain curve as the number of repetitions increases, being initially concave to the strain axis and becoming convex as the stiffness decreases. This is illustrated in Figure 2.7.

Concrete is not homogeneous and fatigue of concrete is a progressive process of microcrack initiation and propagation leading to macrocracks which can grow and determine the remaining fatigue life by causing stress to increase until failure occurs. The important characteristics of the fatigue process are the stress/strain changes under cyclic loading and the related mechanics of crack growth. Research at Lehigh University by Assimacopoulos et al.(1959) showed that failure tended to occur at the matrix-aggregate interface, at any rate in the case of 9 mm sandstone and quartzite gravel. Kaplan (1962,1965), considering crack formation and growth under static loading, suggested that the beginning of the failure process was marked by the formation of

12

multiple cracks in the mortar with the aggregate forming a barrier. He associated the cracking with the release of strain energy and it is reasonable to assume repeated loading is similar. Glucklich (1965) studied the effect of microcracking on creep and fatigue using mortar beams tested in flexure. Working on ideas originally proposed by Griffith (1922), Glucklich found that the critical crack length to cause fatigue failure agreed closely with that for static conditions in terms of the critical strain energy release rate. It appears that the mechanism of fatigue in concrete starts with the breakdown of bond between the cement matrix and the aggregate. This is followed by the progression of cracking through the mortar, arrested when it meets a stone until the process is repeated. When the strain energy so released overcomes the remaining cohesive forces in the concrete complete fracture results.

Since 1985 the whole field of research on fatigue of reinforced concrete has been reviewed by CEB General Task Group 15 whose State-of-the Art Report, Bulletin No. 188 was published in 1988.

Experimental cyclic compressive stress-strain relations have been determined and mathematical models derived by Sinha, Gerstle and Tulin (1964).

Sinha et al (1964) developed expressions for the envelope curve of the so called post-peak cycles. Similar work for tensile cycles was reported by Reinhardt, Cornelissen and Hordijk (1986).

Post-peak curves for concrete in tension relate crack opening to stress and are important in the application of non-linear fracture mechanics to concrete. A softening zone of microcracking develops in front of a macrocrack and stresses are transferred depending on the size of the crack opening which causes the non-elastic deformation. This is illustrated in Figure 2.2 and described further in Appendix 2.

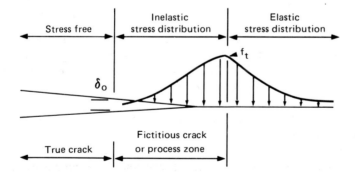

Fig. 2.2
Tensile stress distribution in front of a crack in concrete (Reinhardt, Cornelissen and Hordijk, 1986, CEB Bulletin No.188)

The softening process caused by the microcracking absorbs energy and Tepfers, Hedberg and Szczekocki (1984) have reported a method of predicting fatigue damage and life through energy absorption by summing hysteresis of the cycles.

Figure 2.3 due to Holmen (1979) shows a comparison of developing damage during cyclic loading as detected by the different methods mentioned in Chapter 1.

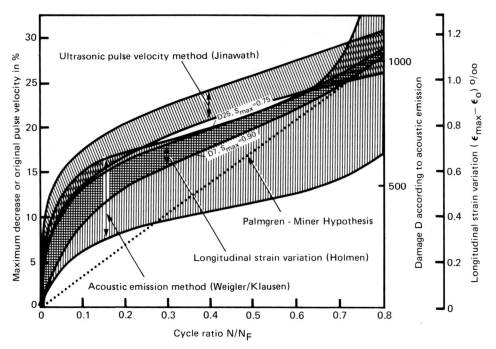

Fig. 2.3
Development of fatigue damage
(Holmen, 1979, CEB Bulletin No.188)

Later workers found that S-N curves for concrete in tension were similar to those for compression. Some work was done with eccentric compressive loading which suggested a gain in fatigue strength of 17 per cent compared with axial compression.

Time dependent effects such as specimen age, frequency of cyclic loading and the benefits of rest periods had been studied but Raithby and Whiffen (1968) were unable to interpret the results on a common basis or over a sufficient range of endurances. Their review pointed the need for a coordinated programme of research to cover the whole range of significant parameters such as the range of concrete mixes in use, the effects of spectrum loading and a fuller understanding of the mechanism of fatigue failure.

2.2 Fatigue strength and deformation

The fatigue strength of concrete that can be sustained for a given number of repetitions is commonly expressed as a fraction of the static compressive strength, f_{cm}. Figure 2.4 shows typical S-N curves with experimental data for concrete in compression.

These lines have been plotted for constant $\sigma_{min} = 0.2f_{cm}$ but S-N lines may also be prepared for constant ratio, $R = \sigma_{min}/\sigma_{max}$ as exemplified by Figure 2.5

14

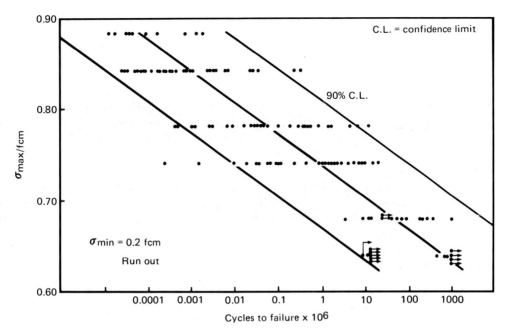

Fig. 2.4
Typical S-N lines, concrete in compression
(Klausen, 1978, CEB Bulletin No.188)

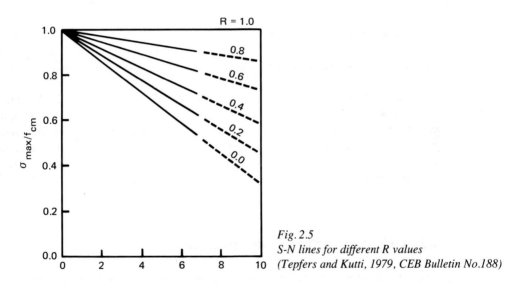

Fig. 2.5
S-N lines for different R values
(Tepfers and Kutti, 1979, CEB Bulletin No.188)

It can be seen that for a given number of cycles a higher σ_{min} results in a higher $\sigma_{max.}$ From the work of Aas-Jakobsen (1970) and Tepfers and Kutti (1979) the above relationship has been expressed in the equation:

$$\sigma_{max}/f_{cm} = 1 - \beta(1 - R)\log N$$

where $R=\sigma_{min}/\sigma_{max}$ and β is a material constant with a value from 0.064 to 0.080.

15

Work by Siemes (1983) showed that most of the scatter in S-N curves for concrete can be explained by the variability of the static strength, f_c

Holmen (1979) studied longitudinal strain variations during compression fatigue tests and found the total strain developed as shown in Figure 2.6 which is of the same form as Figure 2.3. Short duration tests showed that strains were directly related to stress and relatively independent of the number of cycles to failure, N.

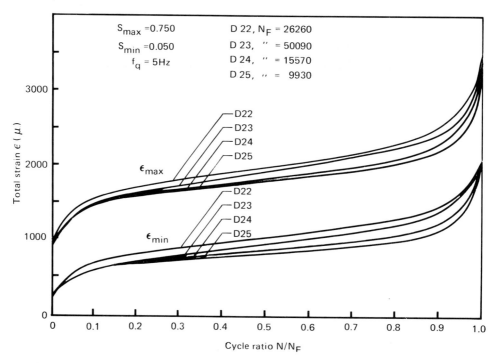

Fig. 2.6
Development of cyclic strain
(Holmen, 1979, CEB Bulletin No.188)

The total maximum strain has two components: $\varepsilon_{max} = \varepsilon_e + \varepsilon_t$, where ε_e is related to endurance and includes elastic strain and ε_t is time dependent and analogous to creep. In general, strain develops in three stages: a rapid increase up to about 10 per cent of total life, a second uniform increase from 10 to about 80 per cent and finally a rapid increase to failure. Figure 2.7 shows changing cyclic stress-strain curves recorded by Holmen which confirmed Van Ornum's observations. The development of strain should provide the means of assessing remaining life and ultimate strain could be a criterion for fatigue failure.

Guolee (1983) suggested that residual strain might be used as a parameter to measure fatigue damage. Sparks (1982) realised the importance of the secondary (uniform) stage and derived equations relating the rate of change of strain per cycle to the number of cycles to failure.

16

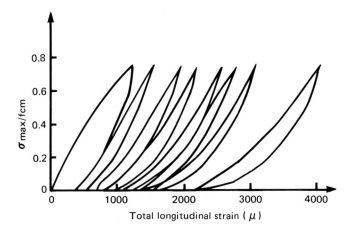

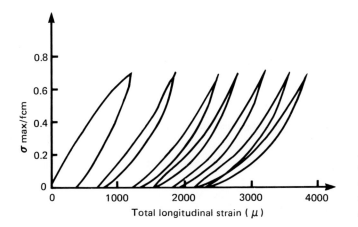

Fig. 2.7
Cyclic stress/strain curves for
concrete in compression
(Holmen, 1979, CEB Bulletin
No.188)

$$\log N = -2.66 - 0.94 \log\varepsilon'_{cyc} \text{ for gravel concrete.}$$

$$\log N = -3.79 - 1.06 \log\varepsilon'_{cyc} \text{ for Lytag concrete.}$$

Holmen (1979) also observed the increase in elastic strain with the number of repetitions and the reduction in secant modulus shown in Figure 2.8.

So far the foregoing review relates to concrete in compression - its principal structural function. However its fatigue properties under repeated tensile stresses are also important as affecting its susceptibility to cracking. Some fatigue tests on lean concrete by Kolias and Williams (1978) indicated fatigue strength, expressed as a fraction ot static strength, similar to that obtained by Raithby in a considerable number of flexural tests reported by him (1979) in "Behaviour of concrete under fatigue loading". It can be

17

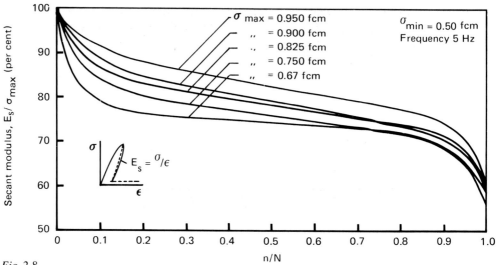

Fig. 2.8

Change of secant modulus of elasticity
(Holmen, 1979, CEB Bulletin No.188)

concluded that the effects on fatigue strength of parameters such as mix design, age of concrete and moisture content are similar for compressive, flexural and tensile loading. Numerous splitting tests on concrete cubes by Tepfers (1979) led to the following equation:

$$\sigma_{max}/f_{csplm} = 1 - \beta \,(1 - R) \log N$$

where $R = \sigma_{min}/\sigma_{max}$ and $\beta = 0.0685$

This is similar to the equation for compression with one suggested value of β.

Saito and Imai (1983) found that the stress-strain diagrams are almost linear and although their slope hardly changes throughout the fatigue life the residual strain steadily increases to about 120 microstrain at the beginning of failure. This is illustrated in Figure 2.9.

Cornelissen and Reinhardt (1984) obtained similar results and gave special attention to the development of tensile cyclic strain rate, ε'_{cyc}, which they found correlated strongly with the number of cycles to failure as shown in Figure 2.10.

Their equation:

$$\log N = -3.25 - 0.89 \log \varepsilon'_{cyc} \text{ for a testing frequency of 6 Hz}$$

is very similar to that obtained by Sparks (1982) from compression fatigue tests. A more general form gives the time in seconds to failure:

$$\log t_f = -4.02 - 0.89 \log \varepsilon'_{cyc}$$

18

which is of the same type as the relation found by Sparks and Menzies (1973) for concrete in compression. Cornellissen and Reinhardt (1984) also verified the validity of the Palmgren-Miner summation with a failure criterion of $\Sigma n/N \leq 1$.

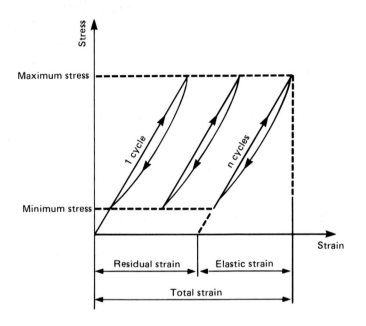

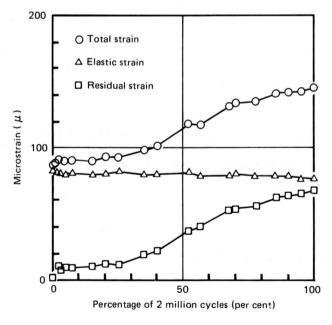

Fig. 2.9
Development of tensile strain
components
(Saito and Imai, 1983, CEB
Bulletin No.188)

19

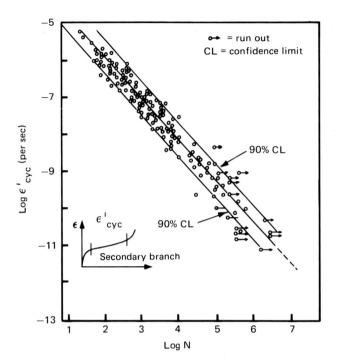

Fig. 2.10
Correlation between tensile cyclic strain rate and fatigue life
(Cornelissen and Reinhardt, 1984, CEB Bulletin No.188)

To study the effect of stress reversal, Murdock and Kesler (1958) conducted flexural tests the results of which, with results of other investigators, suggested that stress reversals did not reduce fatigue strength. Tepfers (1982) investigated reversals by means of cube splitting tests with precompression in the splitting plane but the results showed so much scatter that there was no cogent conclusion. However there has been more convincing work, notably that of Cornelissen and Reinhardt (1984), to suggest that stress reversals do tend to reduce tensile fatigue strength as shown by the S-N curves of Figure 2.11.

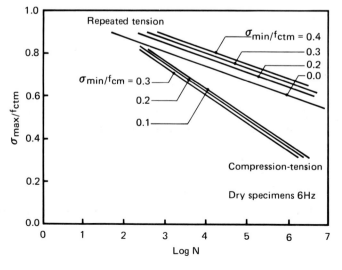

Fig. 2.11
Detrimental effect of stress reversals
(Cornelissen and Reinhardt, 1984, CEB Bulletin No.188)

20

Cornelissen and Siemes (1985) developed the following S-N equation for reversed stress cycles leading to tensile failure:

$$\log N = 8.94 - 7.68\sigma_{max}/f_{cm} - 0.37\sigma_{min}/f_{cm}$$

For reversed stress cycles with dominant compression and compression failure they proposed the following S-N relation:

$$\log N = 1.58 \, (\sigma_{min}/f_{cm})^{-3.14}$$

The results of their repeated tension and alternating compression-tension tests are shown in the modified Goodman diagram, Figure 2.12.

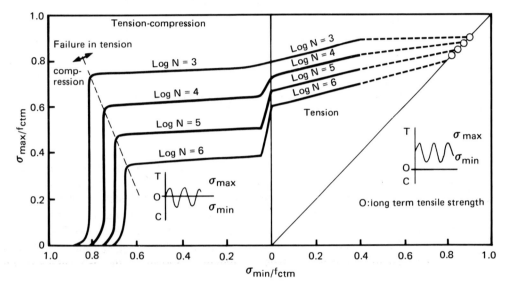

Fig. 2.12
Modified Goodman diagrams
(Cornelissen and Siemes, 1985, CEB Bulletin No.188)

The detrimental effect of compression on tensile fatigue strength is supported by bending tests at the Magnel Laboratory reported by Cornelissen (1984) in Heron from which typical S-N curves are shown in Figure 2.13.

Work by Rings (1986) demonstrated the reduction in compression fatigue strength due to even quite low tensile stresses in the cycles. This is summarised in the modified Goodman diagram of Figure 2.14.

Typical stress-strain curves for concrete subjected to stress reversal are shown in Figure 2.15. The early cycles produce a compressive strain which remains more or less constant whilst tensile strain increases at maximum tensile stress leading to hysteresis and failure.

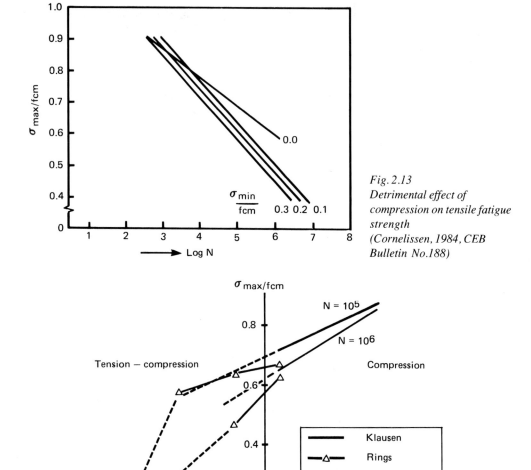

Fig. 2.13
*Detrimental effect of
compression on tensile fatigue
strength
(Cornelissen, 1984, CEB
Bulletin No.188)*

Fig. 2.14
*Compressive fatigue strength reduced by tensile stresses
(Rings, 1986, CEB Bulletin No.188)*

It has been noted that fatigue test results are subject to considerable scatter and therefore call for statistical evaluation. McCall (1958) suggested a method to express S-N relations in terms of the probabilities of failure, P, as instanced in Figures 2.16 and 2.17

Holmen (1979),Van Leeuwen and Siemes (1979) showed that the scatter in fatigue compression tests can be attributed mainly to the scatter in static compressive strength, f_{cm}. Raithby (1979) in "Flexural fatigue behaviour of plain concrete" made similar

22

observations from flexural tests. Cornelissen and Reinhardt (1984) found similarly for tension and compression-tension as shown in Figure 2.18.

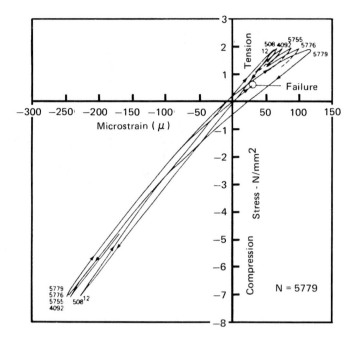

Fig. 2.15
Cyclic stress/strain curves for reversals
(Cornelissen and Reinhardt, 1984, CEB Bulletin No.188)

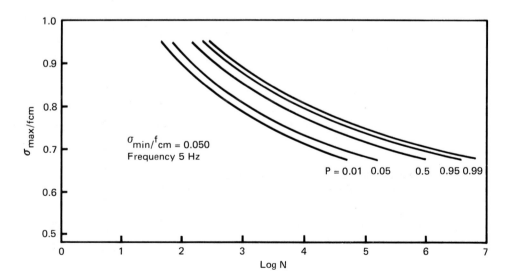

Fig. 2.16
Compressive S-N probabilities
(Holmen, 1979, CEB Bulletin No.188)

23

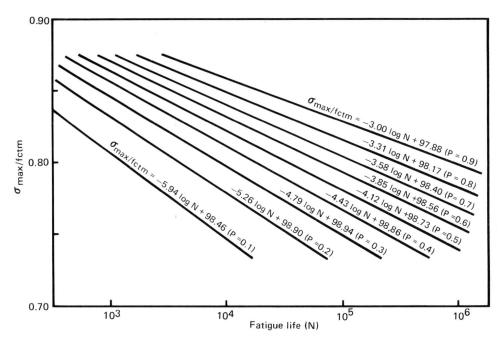

Fig. 2.17
Tensile S-N probabilities
(Saito and Imai, 1983, CEB Bulletin No.188)

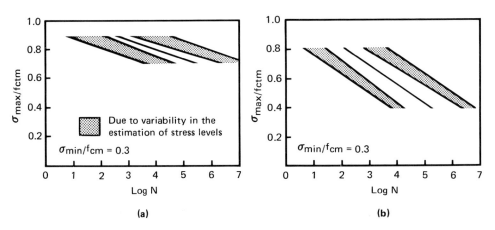

(a)   **(b)**

Fig. 2.18
Scatter in S-N due to variation in estimating stress
(Cornelissen and Reinhardt, 1984, CEB Bulletin No.188)

2.3 Concrete composition and moisture content

2.3.1 Concrete composition

Parameters such as water-cement ratio, cement content, air entrainment, curing conditions and age of concrete do not have to be taken into account separately provided fatigue strength is expressed in terms of static strength. Raithby (1979) established this convincingly in a programme testing several hundred plain concrete beams 102mm square and 510mm long. Two types of pavement quality concrete and a lean concrete mix were as defined in Table 2.1.

TABLE 2.1

Concrete mixes

Mix	PQ1	PQ2	LC1
Aggregate	Flint	Limestone	Flint
Mean 28 day cube strength (N/mm²)	44.8	33.3	21.0

Figure 2.19, from the work of Galloway, Harding and Raithby (1979) at TRRL, is a typical fatigue curve showing the scatter in the results of tests on mix PQ1.

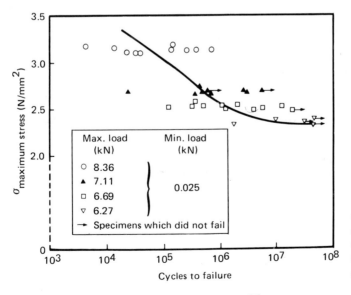

Fig. 2.19
S-N curve for saturated concrete
(Galloway, Harding and Raithby, 1979, LR 864)

Figure 2.20, from the same source, plots the results from tests on the three different mixes to indicate a single relationship regardless of age when each maximum cycle stress is divided by the appropriate flexural strength.

From tests on laboratory dry cubes, Tepfers and Kutti (1979) found the fatigue characteristics of lightweight concrete to be comparable with those of normal weight concrete. Uniaxial tensile tests on saturated cylinders by Saito (1984) suggested that lightweight concrete had rather higher fatigue strength than normal concrete having the same static strength as shown in Figure 2.21.

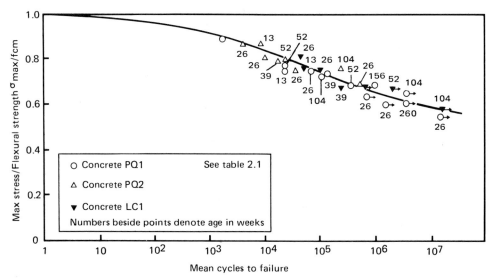

Fig. 2.20
S-N curve in terms of static flexural strength
(Raithby, 1979, ASP)

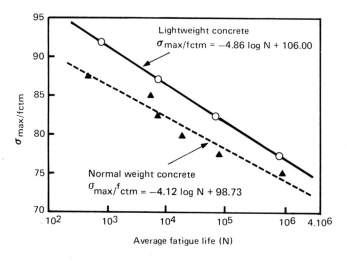

Fig. 2.21
Tensile S-N curves for normal and lightweight concrete
(Saito, 1984, CEB Bulletin No.188)

On the other hand, similar tests reported by Cornelissen (1987 supplement to 1984 work) gave results for lightweight concrete which were about the same as S-N curves for normal concrete with axial tension but rather lower with alternating compression-tension as shown in Figure 2.22.

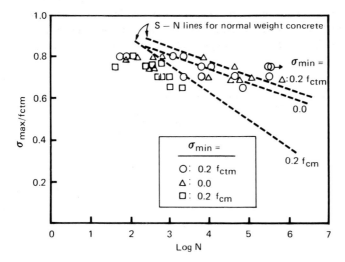

Fig. 2.22
Tensile and compressive-tensile S-N curves for normal and lightweight concrete (Cornelissen, 1984,1987, CEB Bulletin No.188)

Compressive fatigue tests by Waagaard (1981,1986) suggested that lightweight concrete was superior to normal concrete. In view of these conflicting results, it seems reasonable generally to assume their fatigue strengths in terms of static ultimate strengths are about the same unless there is other evidence.

See also 5.2.4 where it is noted that cracks may pass through some lightweight aggregate particles rather than around them. The strength of aggregate per se is therefore significant.

2.3.2   Moisture content

Galloway, Harding and Raithby (1979) reported on the effects of moisture on the fatigue process. Mix PQ1 concrete beams were cured under water for 26 weeks. Randomly selected groups were then treated differently as follows:

1   Drying out prevented by sealing in polythene with free water - Saturated

2   Allowed to dry at room temperature - Surface dry

3   Oven dried for one week at 105°C,allowed to cool,then sealed - Oven dry

4   Some oven dry beams were soaked for three weeks,then sealed - Resoaked

The mean static flexural strength of the surface dry beams was 21 per cent lower than that of the saturated beams. Loss of strength due to partial drying was reported by

Walker and Bloem (1957) who showed that the loss was related to the drying time; they found a loss of 40 per cent after 4 days but half of this was regained at 32 days.

The mean static flexural strength of oven dry specimens was about 50 per cent higher than that of saturated specimens which contrasts with a 40 per cent reduction as a result of oven drying observed by Mills (1960).

Resoaking the oven dry specimens replaced most of the evaporable water but the mean static flexural strength only reverted from 50 to 25 per cent. This result conflicts with the findings of Walker and Bloem (1957) and Mills (1960).

The results of the TRRL fatigue tests are shown in Figure 2.23 and followed the trend of the TRRL static flexural strength tests. The saturated beam tests showed the least scatter.

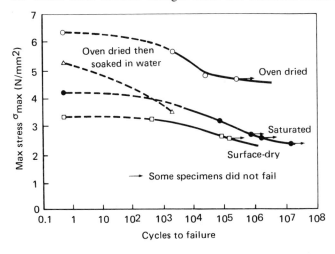

Fig. 2.23
S-N curves for different
moisture states
(Galloway, Harding and
Raithby, 1979, LR 864)

Equivalent cube strength tests were carried out on the broken test pieces. There was no correlation between strength and previous stress history - whether the beam had failed under static or fatigue loading. The results were aggregated and strength near fracture is plotted against strength near end of beam in Figure 2.24. This shows a statistically significant 2 per cent reduction in strength near the fracture, probably due to micro-cracking.

The mean compressive strengths of the surface dry and oven dry beams were respectively 12 and 16 per cent higher than that of the saturated beams. However the resoaked beams had 18 per cent lower strengths probably due to differential expansion as water was reabsorbed into the pore structure as suggested by Mills (1960). The oven dry beams suffered a more explosive type of failure than the others.

The sensitivity of flexural, fatigue and compressive strength to moisture conditions underlines the importance of considering the moisture conditions of structures in service when assessing their performance. For instance, in the United Kingdom, concrete road slabs are likely to register more than 85 per cent humidity for most of the year except at the upper surface whilst bridges are subject to much wider variations of moisture content.

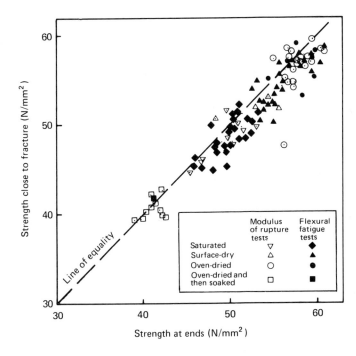

Fig. 2.24
Concrete strength close to
fracture planes
(Galloway, Harding and
Raithby, 1979, LR 864)

The flexural tests were in 4-point bending. Static loading was applied at a standard rate of 2.67 kN/min, equivalent to a rate of increase of surface stress of 0.017 N/mm²s. Fatigue loading was applied at 20 Hz with zero minimum stress.

2.3.3   Curing

As moisture content has such a significant effect on the strength, stiffness and fatigue performance of beams cured by immersion in water for 26 weeks, the TRRL research was extended by Galloway, Harding and Raithby (1979) to study the effect of different curing methods on these properties. Variants of three types of curing regime, all at 20C, were   investigated:

1   Different combinations of water immersion and air curing.

2   Fog room at 95 per cent relative humidity.

3   Use of curing membranes.

The air curing was at 65 per cent relative humidity except for one series of tests in which the humidity varied from 41 to 75 per cent with an average of 57 per cent and the results were virtually the same. The total curing time for all beams was 26 weeks and the full 26 weeks immersion in water was taken as the basis of comparisons.

Figure 2.25 shows that the beams immersed in water gained 0.64 per cent of their original weight in the first week, 0.74 per cent by the fourth week and 0.93 per cent at the end of 26 weeks. In this time those in the fog room gained 0.60 per cent and by contrast those exposed to the air lost up to 3 per cent by evaporation. The effectiveness of the membranes varied considerably. Polyethylene limited the weight loss to 0.2 per cent, wax coating to more than 1 per cent whilst coating with sodium silicate did virtually nothing to stop evaporation.

The results of length measurements are given in Figure 2.26. Most of the expansion following immersion takes place in the first 2 or 3 weeks. After removal from the water,

Curve	Time in water (weeks)	Time in air (weeks)
A	13	13
B	4	22
C	1	25
D	0	26 silicate coated
E	0	26 constant RH

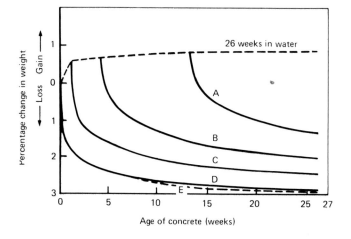

Fig. 2.25
Effect of immersion time on weight
(Galloway, Harding and Raithby, 1979, LR 864)

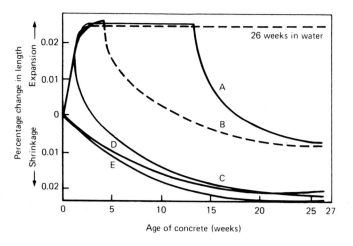

Fig. 2.26
Effect of immersion time on length
(Galloway, Harding and Raithby, 1979, LR 864)

shrinkage proceeds at reducing rates like evaporation. The final shrinkage of the air-cured beams was similar to that of the ones immersed for 1 week only and about three times that of the beams which had been immersed for 4 and 13 weeks. Thus early shrinkage and loss of moisture are considerably delayed by initial immersion in water. The products of hydration during immersion restrict subsequent moisture movement, resist shrinkage and influence the strength of the concrete.

Evaporation after removal from water results in a reduction in density as shown in Figure 2.27 together with the variations in strength and moduli.

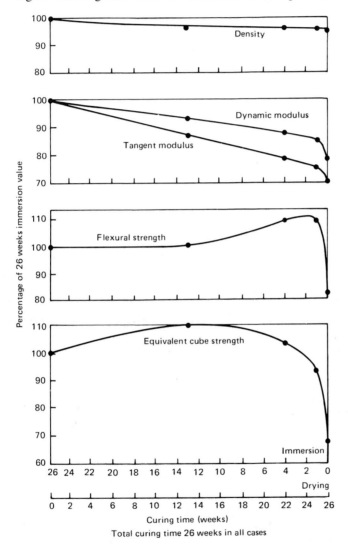

Fig. 2.27
Effect of immersion and drying times (Galloway, Harding and Raithby, 1979, LR 864)

The highest flexural strengths were obtained by 1 or 4 weeks immersion followed by 25 and 22 weeks of air-drying respectively. This strength was about 10 per cent higher than that of beams immersed for 13 or 26 weeks. The air-cured beams with no immersion had strengths about 20 per cent lower than the water-cured beams. The surface coated beams

31

were about 15 per cent weaker and those cured in the fog room were about 7 per cent weaker than the water-cured beams.

The flexural strength of beams which had been subjected to previous fatigue loading was generally higher than those which had not. The nominal cyclic tensile stresses were 3.22 N/mm^2 maximum and zero minimum at 20 Hz.

The maximum stress was 61 to 81 per cent of the original mean flexural strength. This may suggest that repeated stressing, provided that it is not high enough to propagate any existing cracks, actually strengthens the concrete by plastic deformation and relief of stress concentrations.

Similar effects have been recorded under compressive stresses by Bennett and Raju (1971). However the beams which had survived 5 to 12 million cycles of fatigue loading could have been above average strength and therefore would have had higher than average residual strength.

The variations in equivalent cube strength and elastic moduli in Figure 2.27 did not correlate with flexural strength but the values for the air-cured beams were some 30 and 20 per cent lower than those for the water-cured ones.

The fatigue endurance of the various groups of beams followed the trend of the differences in flexural strength. Dividing the maximum fatigue stress by the corresponding flexural strength provided values which are plotted in Figure 2.28 to suggest a single S-N curve. This could be used to predict fatigue behaviour if flexural strength is known.

The variation in maximum tensile strain with the number of loading cycles for typical examples of the different curing methods is shown in Figure 2.29. The strain increases very gradually over most of the life but increases very rapidly in the last few hundred cycles.

Tests by Van Leeuwen and Siemes (1979) with repeated compressive stress cycles showed that wet concrete was inferior to dry concrete as shown in Figure 2.30

Waagaard (1981) reported that dry concrete specimens endured 10 to 100 times more stress cycles than wet specimens, everything else being equal. Similar trends were found for tensile stresses by Cornelissen and Reinhardt (1984).

2.4 Loading effects

2.4.1 Rate of loading

Galloway and Raithby (1973) reviewed early work from which the rate of loading was found to have an appreciable effect on the flexural strength of concrete and mortar

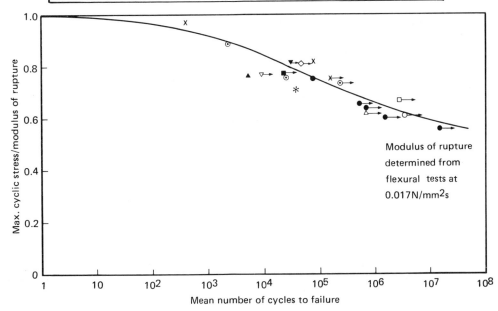

Fig. 2.28
Fatigue performance in terms of modulus of rupture
(Galloway, Harding and Raithby, 1979, LR 864)

beams, notably that of McHenry and Schideler (1955), Wright (1964) and Lloyd, Lott and Kesler (1968). Therefore it might be expected that fatigue performance would be dependent upon the frequency of loading. However reports by Raithby and Whiffen (1968) and Kesler (1953) have indicated no significant difference in fatigue life for frequencies between 0.5 Hz and 7.5 Hz.

Galloway and Raithby (1973) investigated the relationship between flexural strength and the rate of increase of extreme fibre stress in small beams using two concrete mixes. Their results are summarised in Figure 2.31.

The rate of loading in a fatigue test at 20 Hz, 172 N/mm²s, is about 10,000 times that in a standard flexural strength test, 0.0172 N/mm²s. This increase was found to increase the modulus of rupture by about 50 per cent in the case of both of the concrete mixes tested. PQ1 mix beams were tested both wet and dry at 4 Hz and 20 Hz and it was concluded that any differences in fatigue performance were due to moisture state and strength and not the rate of loading. This is illustrated in Figure 2.32.

The maximum stress levels were less than 75 per cent of the static flexural strength in

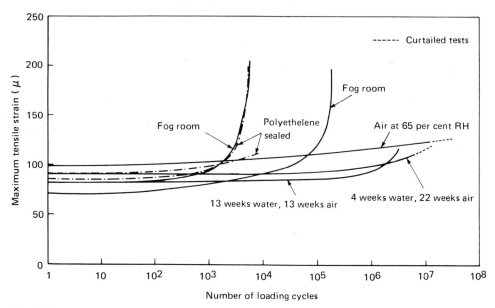

Fig. 2.29
Variation of tensile strain
(Galloway, Harding and Raithby, 1979, LR 864)

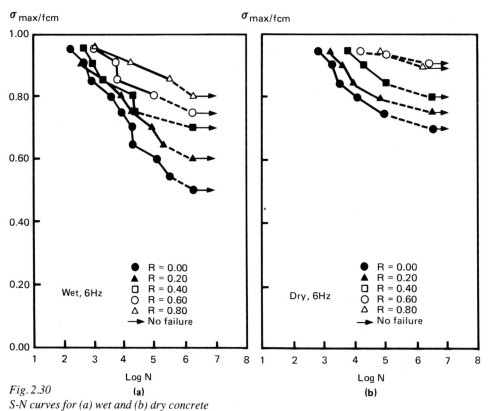

Fig. 2.30
(a)
S-N curves for (a) wet and (b) dry concrete
(Van Leeuwen and Siemes, 1979, CEB Bulletin No.188)

34

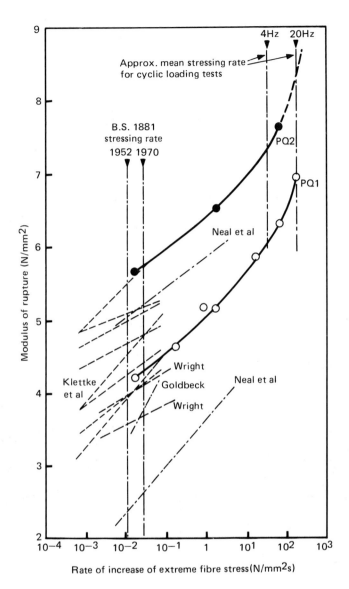

Fig. 2.31
Modulus of rupture versus
rate of loading
(Galloway and Raithby, 1973,
LR 547)

the tests that led to the above result. At higher stress levels McCall(1958),Galloway and Raithby (1973) and Holmen (1979) found that fatigue strength increases with increasing frequency. Sparks and Menzies (1973) did compressive fatigue tests on concrete prisms which showed that an increase in frequency from 0.6 Hz to 6 Hz resulted in only a tenfold increase in the number of cycles to failure. A comparison by Van Leeuwen and Siemes (1979) showed that the increase in loading frequency from 0.7 Hz to 6 Hz results in more cycles to failure at the same stress level but, as the increase in N is considerably less than ninefold, the fatigue life decreases in time units. Similar observations were made by Cornelissen (1984) for concrete in uniaxial tension and compression-tension at 6 Hz and 0.6 Hz.

Thus accelerated fatigue tests on concrete may well overestimate the true fatigue life of a structure that carries high cycle stresses at lower rates in service. High frequency

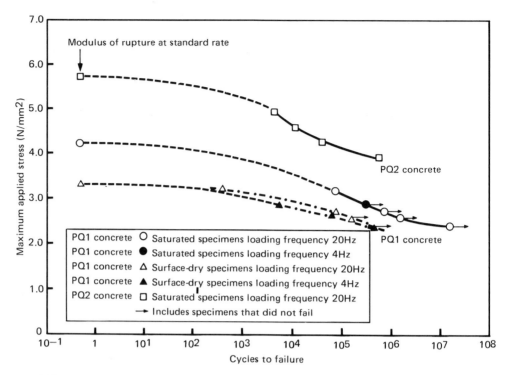

Fig. 2.32
Different moisture states and rates of loading
(Galloway and Raithby, 1973, LR 547)

testing may cause undesirable heating. For instance Lascheidt (1965) recorded a temperature rise of 8°C in reinforced concrete tested at 11 Hz due either to rib interaction or hysteresis in the concrete.

A theoretical study of the effect of frequency on fatigue by Hsu (1981) introduced the period time, T, and defined low-cycle and high-cycle fatigue by means of the transition equation:

$$\log N = 3 - 0.353 \log T$$

Thus for frequency 1 Hz, T = 1 and N = 1000 so high-cycle and low-cycle are defined for values of N respectively above and below 1000. For 6Hz N = 1882.

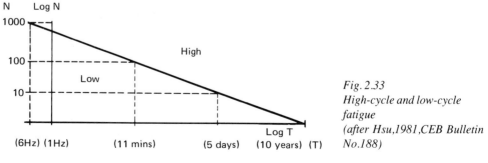

Fig. 2.33
High-cycle and low-cycle
fatigue
(after Hsu,1981,CEB Bulletin
No.188)

36

Other implications are shown in Figure 2.33.

Hsu developed the S-N equations of Tepfers and Kutti (1979) for low-cycle fatigue:

$$\sigma_{max}/f_{cm} = 1.20 - 0.20R - 0.133(1 - 0.779R)\log N - 0.053(1 - 0.445R)\log T$$

and for high-cycle fatigue he proposed:

$$\sigma_{max}/f_{cm} = 1 - 0.0662(1 - 0.556R)\log N - 0.0294\log T$$

in which $R = \sigma_{min}/\sigma_{max}$

2.4.2   Rest periods

The effect of rest periods was studied by Hilsdorf and Kesler (1966) by fatigue tests on plain concrete in flexure. Rest periods up to 5 minutes after each block of 4500 loading cycles seemed to allow the concrete to recover and raise fatigue strength. In a limited series of flexural tests Raithby and Galloway (1974) imposed a rest of up to 2 seconds after each loading cycle but high scatter made the results statistically inconclusive. Siemes (1985) carried out tests in which either σ_{max} or σ_{min} was held constant for periods between 1.5 and 10 minutes. There was a small improvement but it was not significant because of scatter. Longer rest periods allowing redistribution of stress and healing may result in longer fatigue lives if the stress in the rest period is sufficiently low.

2.4.3   Preloading and remnant strength

CEB Bulletin No. 188, Section 3.10, states that strength and stiffness are affected by loading history. Fatigue strength of concrete is defined as the fraction of static strength that it can sustain for a certain number of cycles to failure. However the static strength of a specimen which has undergone a given number of cycles cannot be used to quantify the amount of damage it has suffered. The Palmgren-Miner linear damage rule does not coincide with the development of actual damage. This rule relates to the ultimate near failure state and not to intermediate changes in strength or stiffness. Awad and Hilsdorf (1974) have shown that N_p cycles of compressive preloading of concrete up to N_p/N about 0.2 to 0.3 enhances its static compressive strength but preloading continued to higher N_p/N ratios had a detrimental effect as shown in Figure 2.34.

Cook and Chindaprasirt (1980), Sri Ravindrarajah (1982), Tinec and Bruhwiler(1985) and Cornelissen and Reinhardt (1986) conducted static and repeated preloading tests. Whilst static compressive preloading improves stiffness by a consolidating effect, cyclic preloading is generally detrimental to stiffness and reloading strength, the worst case being cyclic tensile preloading.

2.4.4 Other special loading effects

Kronen and Andersen (1983) carried out a few compressive fatigue tests at cryogenic

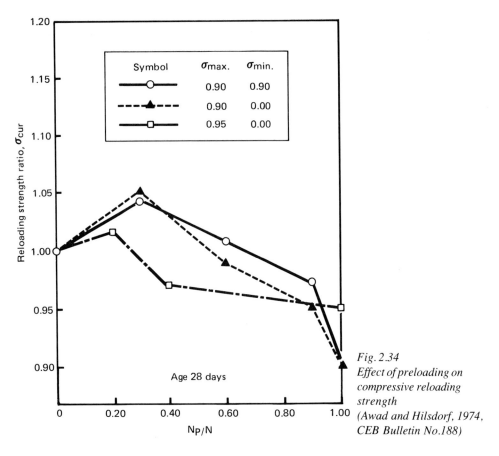

Fig. 2.34
Effect of preloading on compressive reloading strength
(Awad and Hilsdorf, 1974, CEB Bulletin No.188)

temperature, minus 196°C, on saturated concrete at 10 Hz. Both fatigue strength and static strength increased enormously so the values of σ_{max}/f_c were still comparable with those at room temperature.

Fatigue strength is increased by applying lateral confining pressure. Work has been done by Takhar, Jordaan and Gamble (1974) and Traina and Jeragh (1982) which showed that, by referring the enhanced fatigue strength to the appropriate biaxial static strength, the effect of the confining pressure disappeared.

Eccentric compression loading tests were carried out by Ople and Hulsbos (1966) to simulate the compression zone of a beam. Fatigue strengths were increased due to stress redistribution and, once again, the effect can be nullified by referring the increased fatigue strength to the appropriate fibre stress for eccentric static loading.

It is convenient to conduct fatigue loading tests at constant amplitude but real structures seldom experience this. Work has been done with multi-stage loading to investigate the validity of the Palmgren-Miner hypothesis and results are given in Appendix 4.

2.5 Summary

Concrete has no fatigue limit but, as a rough guide in the absence of firm data, the fatigue strength at 10 million repetitions is about 55 per cent of static compressive strength.

The fatigue process consists essentially of progressive crack initiation and propagation until the last remaining cohesive forces are overcome during the post peak cycles. Mathematical models of the post peak envelopes are important in the fracture mechanics of concrete.

Fatigue strength can be expressed in the equation:

$$\sigma_{max}/f_{cm} = 1 - \beta \,(1 - R)\, \log N$$

in which $0.064 < \beta < 0.080$.

The fatigue strength of concrete follows the same trends in compression, tension, tension-compression and flexural compression. Generally concrete composition does not have to be taken into account provided that fatigue strength is expressed in terms of static strength. Moisture content however can make a difference.

Air dry concrete may be 20 per cent weaker than saturated concrete.

Oven dry concrete may be up to 50 per cent stronger but half of this gain can be lost by resoaking.

Air cured concrete may be 20 to 30 per cent weaker than water cured concrete.

Accelerated fatigue testing may overestimate the fatigue strength of concrete and may give rise to undesirable hysteretic heating effects.

Rest periods at sufficiently low stress may improve fatigue strength.

Static compressive preloading increases fatigue strength.

Generally cyclic preloading is detrimental to fatigue strength but there is some evidence of an improvement due to cyclic compressive preloading provided that N_p/N does not exceed 0.2.

2.6 References

AAS-JAKOBSEN, L (1970) Fatigue of concrete beams and columns. Bulletin No.70-1, Division of Concrete Structures, NTH, Trondheim

ASSIMACOPOULOS,B A, WARNER, R F and EKBERG, C E (1959) High speed fatigue tests on small specimens of plain concrete. Journal Prestressed Concrete Institute, 4(2), pp53-70.

AWAD, M E and HILSDORF, H K (1974) Strength and deformation characteristics of plain concrete subjected to high repeated and sustained loads. Abeles Symposium. Fatigue of concrete. ACI publication SP-41, pp1-13.

BENNETT, E W and RAJU, N J (1971) Effect of understressing on the deformation and strength of plain concrete in compression. Proc. Int. Conf. Mechanical behaviour of materials. Vol.4. Kyoto.

COOK, D J and CHINDAPRASIRT, P (1980) Influence of loading history upon the compressive properties of concrete. Magazine of Concrete Research, v32, No.111, pp89-100.

CORNELISSEN, H A W and REINHARDT, H W (1984) Uniaxial tensile fatigue of concrete under constant amplitude and programme loading. Magazine of Concrete Research, v 36, No.129 pp216-227.

CORNELISSEN, H A W (1984) Constant amplitude tests on plain concrete in uniaxial tension and tension-compression.Stevin Report SR50, Delft University of Technology, pp79.

CORNELISSEN, H A W (1984) Fatigue failure of concrete in tension. Heron, v 29, No. 4, 68pp.

CORNELISSEN, H A W and SIEMES, A J M (1985) Plain concrete under sustained tensile or tensile and compressive fatigue loadings. Proc. BOSS Conference. Elsevier Science Publishers B. V., Amsterdam, pp487-498.

CORNELISSEN, H A W and REINHARDT, H W (1986) Effect of static and fatigue preloading on residual strength and stiffness of plain concrete. Proceedings of European Conference on Fracture-6. Fracture control of engineering structures. Amsterdam. Vol.3, pp2087-2103.

GALLOWAY, J W and RAITHBY, K D (1973) Effects of rate of loading on flexural strength and fatigue performance of concrete. TRRL Report LR547.

GALLOWAY, J W, HARDING, H M and RAITHBY, K D (1979) Effects of moisture changes on flexural and fatigue strength of concrete. TRRL Report LR864.

GLUCKLICH, J (1965) The effect of microcracking on time-dependent deformations and the long-term strength of concrete. Int. Conf. on Structure of Concrete.

GRAF, O and BRENNER, E (1934) Versuche zur Ermittlungder Wiederstandsfahigkeit von Beton gegen oftmals wiederholte Belastung. Deutscher Ausschuss fur Stahlbeton. Heft 76 und 83.

GRIFFITH, A A (1922) The phenomena of rupture and flow in solids. Philosophical Transactions, Royal Society of London, Series A,22, pp163-198.

GUOLEE, S (1983) Fatigue behaviour of concrete under constant and varying amplitude repeated loading. Master's Thesis, China Acadamy of Railway Sciences, Beijing. p6.

HILSDORF, H K and KESLER, C E (1966) Fatigue strength of concrete under varying flexural stresses. ACI Journal, Proceedings, v63, No.10, pp1059-1076

HOLMEN,J O (1979) Fatigue of concrete by constant and variable amplitude loading. Bulletin No.79-1. Division of Concrete Structures, NTH, Trondheim.

HSU, T C (1981) Fatigue of plain concrete. ACI Journal, Jul-Aug, pp292-305.

KAPLAN, M F (1961) Crack propagation and the fracture of concrete. Journal American Concrete Inst. 58 No.5.

KAPLAN, M F (1965) Application of fracture mechanics to concrete. Int. Conf. on Structure of Concrete.

KESLER, C E (1953) Effect of speed of testing on flexural fatigue strength of plain concrete. Proc. Highway Research Board, 32.

KLAUSEN, D (1978) Festigkeit und Schadigung von Beton bei haufig wiederholter Beanspruchen. PhD Thesis. University of Technology, Darmstadt.

KOLIAS, S and WILLIAMS, R I T (1978) Cement-bound road materials: strength and elastic properties measured in the laboratory. TRRL Report SR 344.

KRONEN, H and ANDERSEN, J H (1983) Properties of cryogenic concrete. Nordic Concrete Research. Publ.2, ed. Nordic Concrete Federation, pp149-166.

LASCHEIDT, H (1965) On the problem of fatigue strength of steel bars embedded in concrete. PhD Thesis, Aachen.

LLOYD, J P, LOTT, J L and KESLER, C E (1968) Fatigue of concrete. Engineering Experimental Station Bulletin No.499, University of Illinios

McCALL, J T (1958) Probability of fatigue failure of plain concrete. ACI Journal, v 55, pp233-444.

McHENRY, D and SHIDELER, J J (1955) Review of data on effect of speed in mechanical testing of concrete. American Society for Testing Materials. Technical Publication No.185.

MILLS, R H (1960) Strength-maturity relationship for concrete which is allowed to dry. RILEM 1st Symposium on concrete and reinforced concrete in hot countries. Haifa.

MURDOCK, J W and KESLER, C E (1958) Effect of range of stress on fatigue strength of plain concrete beams. ACI Journal, v 30, No 2 pp221-233.

OPLE, F S and HULSBOS, C L (1966) Probable fatigue life of plain concrete with stress gradient. ACI Journal, Proceedings, v63, No.1, pp59-82.

RAITHBY, K D and WHIFFEN, A C (1968) Failure of plain concrete under fatigue loading-A review of current knowledge. Road Research Laboratory Report LR231

RAITHBY, K D and GALLOWAY, J W (1974) Effect of moisture conditions, age and rate of loading on fatigue of plain concrete. Abeles Symposium. Fatigue of concrete. ACI Publication SP-41, pp14-34.

RAITHBY, K D (1979) Behaviour of concrete under fatigue loading. Developments in concrete technology - 1, Applied Science Publishers Ltd pp83-110.

RAITHBY, K D (1979) Flexural fatigue behaviour of plain concrete. Fatigue of engineering materials and structures. Vol.2, pp269-278. Pergamon.

REINHARDT, H W, CORNELISSEN, H A W and HORDIJK, D A (1986) Tensile tests and failure analysis of concrete. Submitted for publication in ASCE Journal

RINGS, K H (1986) Unbewehrter und bewehrter Beton unter haufig wiederholter Wechselbeanspruchung. PhD Thesis, University of Darmstadt, 140pp.

SAITO, M and IMAI, S (1983) Direct tensile fatigue of concrete by the use of friction grips. ACI Journal, Proceedings v 80, No. 5 pp431-438.

SAITO, M (1984) Tensile fatigue strength of lightweight concrete. Int.Journal of Cement Composites and Lightweight Concrete. Vol.6,No.3, pp143-149.

SIEMES, A J M (1983) Fatigue of concrete, Part 1: Compressive stresses IRO-MATS/ CUR Report No.112 (in Dutch with extended English summary), 80pp.

SIEMES, A J M (1985) Fatigue of concrete. MATS Research Report third year. IBBC-TNO, The Netherlands, Jan.

SINHA, B B, GERSTLE, K H and TULIN, L G (1964) Stress-strain relations for concrete under cyclic loading. ACI Journal, pp195-211.

SPARKS, P R and MENZIES, J B (1973) The effect of rate of loading upon the static and fatigue strength of plain concrete in compression. Magazine of Concrete Research, v 25, No.83, pp73-80.

SPARKS, P R (1982) The influence of rate of loading and material variability on the fatigue characteristics of concrete. ACI Publication SP-75, pp331-343.

SRI RAVINDRARAJAH, R (1982) Technical Notes: Additional data on the phenomenon of the effect of presustained loading. International Journal of Cement Composites and Lightweight Concrete. Vol.4, No.4, pp251-252.

TAKHAR, S S, JORDAAN, I J and GAMBLE, B R (1974) Fatigue of concrete under lateral confining pressure. Abeles Symposium. Fatigue of concrete. ACI publication SP-41, pp59-61.

TEPFERS, R and KUTTI, T (1979) Fatigue strength of plain, ordinary and lightweight concrete. ACI Journal, May, pp635-652.

TEPFERS, R (1979) Tensile fatigue strength of plain concrete. ACI Journal,Proceedings v76, No. 8 pp 919-933.

TEPFERS, R (1982) Fatigue of plain concrete subjected to stress reversals. ACI Publication SP-75, pp195-217.

TEPFERS, R, HEDBERG, B and SZCZEKOCKI,G (1984) Absorption of energy in fatigue loading of plain concrete. Materials and Structures,v17,No.97,pp59-64

TINEC, C and BRUHWILER, E (1985) Effect of compressive loads on the tensile strength of concrete at high strain rates. International Journal of Cement Composites and Lightweight Concrete. Vol.7, No.2, pp103-108.

TRAINA, L A and JERAGH, A A (1982) Fatigue of plain concrete subjected to biaxial-cyclical loading. ACI publication SP-75, pp217-235.

VAN LEEUEN, J and SIEMES, A J M (1979) Miner's rule with respect to plain concrete. Heron, v 24, No. 1.

VAN ORNUM, J L (1903) Fatigue of cement products. Trans. Am. Soc. Civil Engineers. 51, 443.

WAAGAARD, K (1981) Fatigue strength of offshore concrete structures. COSMAR Reports PP2-1 and PP2-2.

WAAGAARD, K (1986) Experimental investigations on the fatigue strength of offshore structures. Proc. SINTEF mini-seminar. Fatigue of concrete Report No. STF65A86082, pp 4.1-4.35.

WALKER, S and BLOEM, D L (1957) Effects of curing and moisture distribution on measured strength of concrete. Proc. Highway Research Board, 36.

WRIGHT, P J F (1964) The flexural strength of plain concrete - its measurement and use in designing concrete mixes. DSIR RRL Technical Paper No.67, Harmondsworth.

3 Steel reinforcing bars

3.1 Types of steel

The two main types of steel used for concrete reinforcement are mild steel and high yield steel. British Standards specify characteristic strengths of 250 N/mm^2 and 460 N/mm^2 (485 N/mm^2 for hard drawn steel wire) respectively whilst Euronorm 80 establishes three grades: S220, S400 and S500 in which the numbers indicate the minimum yield strength in N/mm^2.

High yield steel may be:

1   Hot rolled alloy steel, or

2   Cold twisted or cold drawn mild steel, or

3   Hardened and tempered steel.

Table 3.1 due to Tilly (1988) gives some particulars.

TABLE 3.1

Typical composition of reinforcing steels

Type	Elements per cent by weight						
	C	Mn	Si	V	Nb	N	
Grade 250 plain round mild steel to BS 4449	0.14/0.19 0.19/0.24	0.55/0.75 0.45/0.55	0.10/0.35				Silicon killed Balanced steel
Cold worked high yield deformed bar to BS 4461 (withdrawn 1988)	0.18/0.23 0.20/0.25	0.60/0.80 0.70/0.90	0.10/0.35				Silicon killed Balanced steel
Hot rolled high yield deformed bar to BS 4449	0.15/0.20 0.18/0.23	1.20/1.25 1.20/1.25	0.25/0.50 0.30/0.50	.005/.008	0.03/0.04	0.012	Silicon killed Nitrovan steel Silicon killed niobium strengthened steel
Autotempered high yield bar (Tempcore)	0.14/0.19 0.11/0.15	0.78/0.98 0.52/0.66	0.03/0.06 0.04/0.05				Product X Product Y

Specifications may designate steel as weldable. The effect of welding on fatigue performance is considered in 3.4.3.

Seventeen cases of fatigue in reinforced concrete are listed in Chapter 1. Although none of these resulted in fracture of the steel and no such case is known to date, it may be necessary to assess the fatigue life of reinforcement because it has to carry an increased cyclic loading or, more commonly, because the concrete has deteriorated and the steel has corroded. The effects of corrosion are considered in 3.5. Moreover it is possible for a reinforcing bar to fail without any signs of distress other than local cracking of the concrete. Fatigue strength is expressed in terms of σ_r, the stress range, and S-N curves are usually plotted as log σ_r against log N.

3.2   Axial fatigue and bending fatigue tests

3.2.1   Background

Research into the behaviour of steel reinforcing bars under fatigue loading has been reviewed by Tilly (1979). Most of the published data was at high stresses and was limited to less than 10 million cycles as illustrated by the typical set of data reported by Tilly and Moss (1982) and plotted in Figure 3.1.

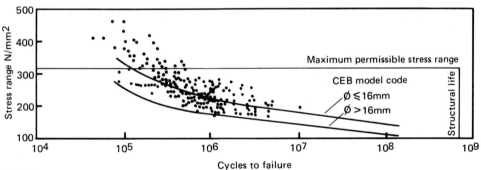

Fig.3.1
Published data in relation to permissible stress range, structural life and CEB-FIP Model Code S-N curves.
(Tilly and Moss,1982,IABSE)

However designs have to be assessed for lower stresses and longer lives than this. For instance British highway bridges have to be checked for a notional life of 120 years which accounts for 700 million cycles and an offshore structure may be subjected to more than 100 million cycles of stress due to wave action in an operational life of 30 years.

Clearly there was a need to update design rules and the CEB-FIP Model Code (1990) S-N curves for bars up to 16 mm and for larger bars are superimposed on Figure 3.1 for comparison. See 6.3.2 for other details. Some of the research which led to these rules will now be reviewed.

45

Moss (1980,1982) reported a comprehensive research programme by TRRL with a constant stress ratio, 0.2, and a number of stress ranges and endurances of 10 million cycles or more.

The two test methods commonly used are axial testing in air and bending tests in concrete beams

3.2.2   Axial fatigue tests

Axial tests can be run at relatively high frequency, up to 150 Hz, so that long endurances can be studied quickly and therefore at relatively low cost. In practice, in the TRRL research programme, the stress ranges up to 200 N/mm^2 were conducted on electro-magnetic resonance machines at 150 Hz, motor driven resonance machines at about 45 Hz and the higher stress range tests were carried out on hydraulic machines at frequencies from 11 to 25 Hz.

Applied stresses can be calculated simply except for complications arising from any eccenticity in clamping the specimen in the testing machine.

The disadvantage of axial testing lies in the method of gripping the test piece which tends to cause high local stress and premature failure at the ends not characteristic of the bar itself. The following interlays have been tried to spread gripping forces evenly:

1   Leather by Yannopoulos and Edwards (1976)

2   Low melting point alloy by Pasko (1973), Walker, Austin, Harrison and Morley (1975),

3   Epoxy resin by Wascheidt (1965)

4   Aluminium   sheet

The standard procedure recommended by RILEM-FIP-CEB requires the free length between grips to be not less than 30 times the nominal diameter, 8 times the pitch of helical ribs (if present) or 500 mm.

Wascheidt (1965) investigated the effect of cladding the bar in concrete and found this made no difference to the endurance of ribbed bars at 11 Hz whilst smooth bars had shorter lives due to interface friction which caused temperature rises of up to 8°C.

3.2.3   TRRL axial tests

Moss (1980) investigated bars of Types A to D, representative of the bars used in structures; mostly they were 16mm diameter but six tests were conducted on 40mm diameter bars of Type A to study the effect of size.

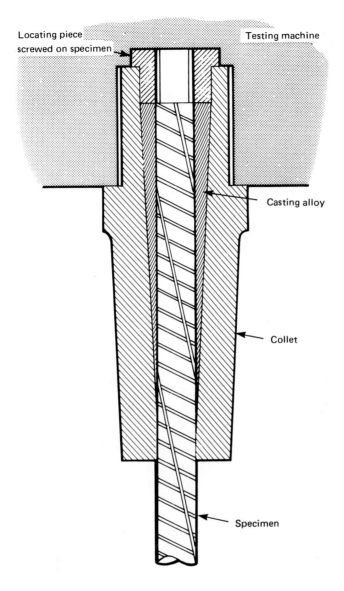

Locating piece
screwed on specimen

Testing machine

Casting alloy

Collet

Specimen

Fig. 3.2
Gripping fixture
(Moss, 1980, SR 622)

The gripping fixture is illustrated in Figure 3.2.

The composition and characteristic strengths of the bars tested are shown in Table 3.2 and their appearance in Figure 3.3. Types A and B were bars cold worked by twisting. Specimens B1 and B2 were of the same type from different sources. Types C and D were hot rolled bars tested as continuous and a welded Type D bar was also tested. Type E was a hot rolled bar with general severe corrosion.

All tests were at constant amplitude except for some narrow band random (NBR) loading tests on 16mm bars of Type A. Further information on NBR loading will be found in Appendix 3. From the constant amplitude results for the 16mm bars shown in

47

Bar type A; Cold worked deformed

Bar type B; Chamfered square twisted

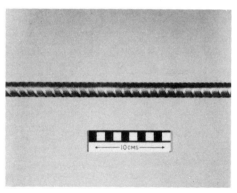

Bar type C; Hot rolled

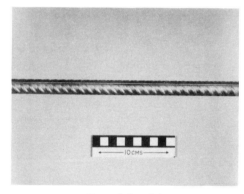

Bar type D; Hot rolled

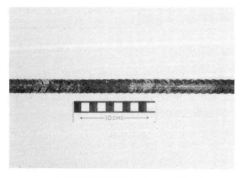

Bar type E. Hot rolled; surface corroded

Fig. 3.3
Appearance of bars tested at TRRL
(Moss, 1980, SR 622)

TABLE 3.2

Properties of bars in TRRL tests

Elements per cent by weight

Type	N/mm²	C	S	P	Si	Mn	Ni	Cr	Mo	V	Cu	Nb	Ti	Al	B	Pb	Sn	Co
	$f_{0.2}$																	
A	460	.20	.032	<.005	.04	.76	.04	.03	<.01	<.01	.07	<.005	<.01	.006	<.001	<.01	<.01	<.01
B1	460	.11	.022	.007	.11	.56	.09	.02	<.01	<.01	.34	<.005	<.01	<.005	<.001	<.01	.02	.02
B2	460	.12	.050	.014	.17	.59	.11	.07	<.01	<.01	.40	<.005	<.01	<.005	<.001	<.01	.04	.01
	f_y																	
C	410	.17	.040	.017	.33	1.38	.10	.07	.02	<.01	.23	.027	<.01	.013	<.001	<.01	.02	<.01
D	460	.24	.029	.020	.27	1.14	.10	.09	.01	.05	.24	<.005	<.01	.011	<.001	<.01	.02	.01
E	-	.33	.018	.030	.43	1.35	.10	.10	.01	<.01	.25	<.005	<.01	.006	<.001	<.01	.05	<.01

Figure 3.4 it can be seen that any minor differences between the types are obscured by scatter although Type D appears to be slightly superior to the others. Figure 3.5 illustrates the lower strengths obtained for 32 and 40mm bars. S-N lines for Classes R1 and R2 (see 3.2.6) are also plotted on Figures 3.4 and 3.5.

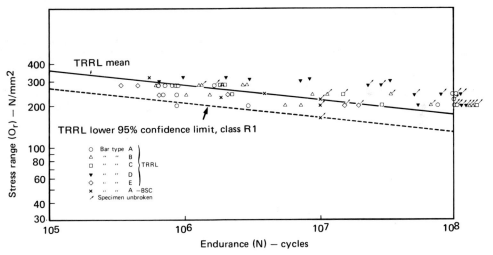

Fig. 3.4
Fatigue performance of 16 mm diameter continuous bars
(Moss, 1980, SR 622)

Failures occurred at endurances up to 97 million cycles and there was no evidence of a fatigue limit. The mean fatigue strength of the Type A 40mm bars was about 30 per cent lower than that of the 16mm bars at 2 million cycles. A regression analysis of the results for the 16mm bars gave the relationship $N(\sigma_r)^{9.5} = K$ where K for the mean line is 1.8×10^{29}

49

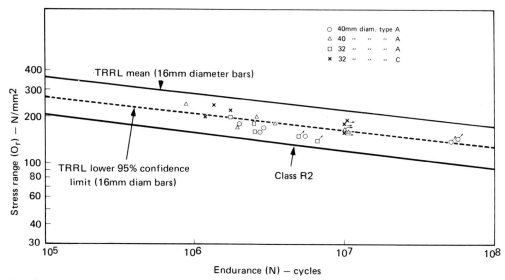

Fig. 3.5
Fatigue performance of large continuous bars
(Moss, 1980, SR 622)

and for the mean minus two standard deviations line K is 1.0×10^{29}. The endurances of the NBR loading tests were found to be longer than those calculated by the Palmgren-Miner damage summation method given in BS 5400. Further information is given in Appendix 4.

The fracture surfaces of a representative selection of specimens were scanned by electron microscope. The significant factor in crack initiation was not the surface rib pattern but surface defects, ranging from 5μm to 100μm in size, associated with the oxide layer. The cold worked bars, Types A and B, had a number of such initiation sites and a helical fracture surface. The hot rolled bars, Types C, D and E, tended to have single crack initiation points and plane fracture surfaces. The general appearance of the fracture surfaces can be seen in Figure 3.6.

3.2.4 Bending fatigue tests

Bending tests in concrete beams are attractive because they simulate the conditions of reinforced concrete in service but they suffer from the disadvantage that cyclic frequencies must be limited to about 3 Hz to avoid heating problems. Generally a single reinforcing bar is cast into a small concrete beam which is tested in 3-point or 4-point bending. To achieve endurances comparable with service requirements the testing machine is occupied for a number of years.

3.2.5   TRRL bending tests

Before starting a comprehensive programme of bending tests, Moss (1982) designed and developed the simple testing machine shown in Figure 3.7.

50

Fig. 3.6
Fracture surfaces
(Moss, 1980, SR 622)

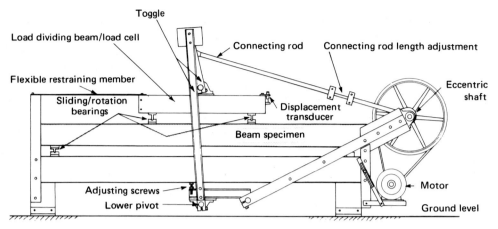

Fig. 3.7
Testing machine (nodding donkey)
(Moss, 1982, SR 748)

The design made use of standard rolled steel sections and readily available stock items to minimise the cost which allowed ten machines to be produced. They functioned successfully for several years as required and became known affectionately as nodding donkeys. Eight of them were kept afterwards for further service. 118 test beams to the design shown in Figure 3.8 were cast using concrete of mean 28 day strength 57.6 N/mm^2 with a standard deviation 3.95 N/mm^2. Three of the bearings provided at loading points and supports permitted longitudinal movement to avoid excessive secondary stresses.

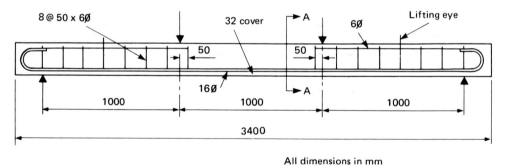

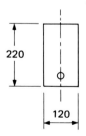

Fig. 3.8
Beam specimen
(Moss, 1982, SR 748)

52

The reinforcing bars tested were all 16mm diameter of Types A,B and C. The test beams were subjected to repeated bending at 3 Hz under constant load amplitude. This necessitated adjustment of the mean displacement in the early stages of the tests until initial cracking had reached a stable state under the cyclic loading. This was typically after about the first 25,000 cycles. In contrast to the axial tests, the strongest factor in crack initiation was the rib pattern. The results are plotted in Figure 3.9 together with the mean line and the mean less two standard deviations line obtained from analysis of these results and also the two lines obtained from the axial fatigue tests. Clearly the bending values in concrete are higher than the axial values in air.

The regression analysis of the bending data came out as $N(\sigma_r)^{8.7} = K$ where K is 0.11×10^{29} for the mean and 0.59×10^{27} for the mean minus two standard deviation. In view of the significant effect of size found in the axial tests some 32mm and 40mm bars were tested and the results of this are given in Figure 3.10.

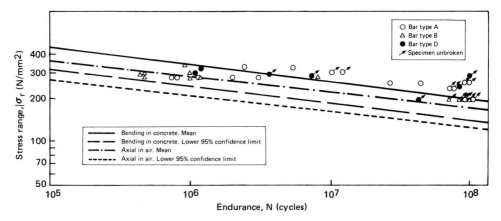

Fig. 3.9
Bending fatigue of 16 mm diameter bars
(Moss, 1982, SR 748)

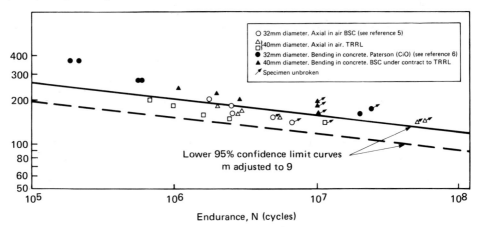

Fig. 3.10
Bending fatigue of 32 mm and 40 mm diameter bars
(Moss, 1982, SR 748)

3.2.6　Conclusions

As all of these lines have very nearly the same slope a simplified intermediate value of 9 was proposed by Tilly and Moss (1982) for the exponent to be used for all types of bar whether tested in air or in concrete. Although the slopes of all of the regression lines can be taken to be the same for practical purposes, it is necessary to use more than one value of K to take account of size. Comparing the results for 16mm bars, performance in terms of stress range is about 20 per cent higher for bending in concrete than axially in air. Assessing fatigue performance on the basis of axial tests in air is therefore likely to be on the safe side and is more convenient.

Using the results of the TRRL work and data from other laboratories S-N curves have been defined by Tilly and Moss (1982) and CEB Bulletin No. 188 (1982), 4.1.4, as follows:

$$2 \text{ million} < N < 10 \text{ million} \quad N \, (\sigma_r)^9 = K \times 10^{27}$$

where K has values for $\emptyset \leq 16$mm and $\emptyset > 16$mm from axial tests of 0.75 and 0.07 respectively.

For $N < 2$ million the σ_r exponent is 6 and for $N > 10$ million an exponent of 11 is appropriate.

The S-N curve for bars up to 16mm is designated Class R1 and that for bigger bars is designated Class R2.

3.3　Surface geometry, size and bending

3.3.1　Surface geometry

Tilly (1979) has described the effects of surface geometry. Deformations are provided to improve bond to concrete but they also cause stress concentrations which reduce fatigue strength. Wascheidt (1965) found the fatigue strength of 16mm diameter ribbed bars was 18 per cent lower than that of smooth round bars for axial tests in air. Snowden (1971) obtained a similar result for bending fatigue of 5.18m long beams. Helgason et al.(1969) found 25mm ribbed bars in concrete beams had a fatigue strength of 190 N/mm^2 at 10 million cycles. 6mm diameter specimens prepared by machining some of the recovered bars had a fatigue strength of 430 N/mm^2 at 10 million cycles when tested in air. However the comparison is not simple because the machining would have removed surface inclusions and other crack initiation sites as well as the ribs but, on the other hand, bending tests in concrete tend to show a higher fatigue strength than axial tests in air.

Wear of the rolls at the steel mills can have an effect. Whilst smoothly worn rolls may tend to form larger base radii which improve fatigue performance, chipped rolls may produce sharp lugs at intervals along the bars which are detrimental. Samples of 32mm bars with a gross defect of this type failed at 2.5 million cycles at 225 N/mm² stress range compared with a sound bar which withstood 300 million cycles at that stress unbroken.

Manufacturer's identification marks can also act as stress raisers. Samples of 16mm bars with badly designed identification marks failed at 2 million cycles at a stress range of 150 N/mm² compared with bars from the same stock without marks which withstood 10 million cycles unbroken.

For bars having longitudinal ribs, their disposition in concrete beams can make a difference. Both Bannister (1969) and Burton and Hognestad (1967) found that ribs in the vertical plane resulted in fatigue strengths as much as 40 per cent lower than was the case for ribs in the horizontal plane. However the TRRL research showed little significant difference between the types of deformed bars tested.

3.3.2   Bar diameter

It was noted (3.2.3) that fatigue strength falls off with increasing size. This effect is not peculiar to reinforcing bars and can be explained by there being a greater likelihood of flaws in a larger surface area. There is a similar effect on static strength.

Frost et al.(1974) found that the effect was no more than 5 per cent for plain round bars from 12mm to 38mm diameter. The effect is much greater for deformed bars as shown in Figure 3.11.

Similar results were reported by Walker et al.(1975) but on the other hand Helgason et al. (1969) found 35mm bars were only about 10 per cent weaker than 16mm bars when tested in concrete beams.

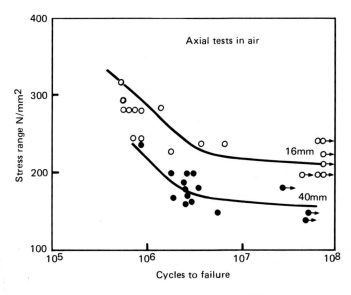

Fig. 3.11
Size effect for Torbar
(Tilly, 1979)

55

Size effect seems to be more pronounced in axial tests than in bending tests. The dominant factor is the relative contributions of crack initiation and crack propagation. In the case of plain bars, most of the fatigue life is crack initiation and propagation time is much the same for all sizes. With deformed bars, initiation is earlier due to the local stress concentrations at the ribs and the subsequent propagation is related to the size of bar.

3.3.3   Bending

In Germany the fatigue strength of ribbed bars is measured by testing bent bars because it gives a conservative value and this is the most demanding condition in which the bars are used. The reduction in fatigue strength increases as the bend (mandrel) diameter,D, decreases relative to the bar diameter,. For Torbar, Nürnberger (1982) found the following reductions at 2 million cycles:

D/σ	Reduction in fatigue strength per cent
25	0
15	16 - 22
10	22 - 41
5	52 - 68

The effect is caused by cold working and residual and bending stresses. High plastic deformation at the inside of a bend reduces the ductility of the steel and increases the incidence of notches. Tensile cracks on the outside of the bend may set up stress concentrations in the concrete but the inside of the bend is critical where residual stresses may be up to 70 per cent of the elastic range. Tensile forces from the straight length of bar cause reversed stresses and concrete deformation. Nürnberger observed that this is where fatigue cracks always initiate.

CEB Bulletin No. 188, 4.1.3.1, proposes two arbitrary classifications:

slightly bent	$D/\sigma \geq 15$	22 per cent reduction
sharply bent	$D/\sigma < 15$	68 per cent reduction

3.4   Connections: lapping, coupling and welding

3.4.1   Lapping

Lapping straight bars with a prescribed minimum overlapping length is the most commonly used and most conservative method of transferring force from one bar to another, in this case through the concrete. The fatigue performance of 12mm lapped

Torbar in concrete beams has been evaluated by Bannister (1978) from 4-point bending tests. He found that lap lengths down to 20 diameters were effective as the bars failed clear of the lap with fatigue strengths no less than the continuous bar. The results are shown in Figure 3.12 with the Class R2 line for comparison.

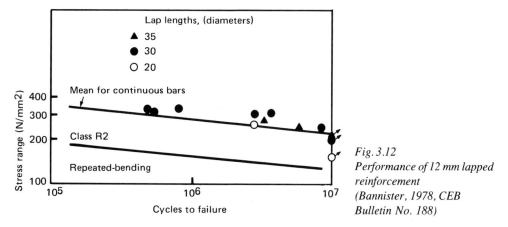

Fig. 3.12
Performance of 12 mm lapped reinforcement
(Bannister, 1978, CEB Bulletin No. 188)

Bennett (1982) showed that cranking bars results in a significant loss of fatigue strength due to stress concentrations.

Davies and Austen (1987) using beam specimens with straight and cranked laps concluded that the straight laps were equivalent in fatigue strength to continuous bars. The cranked laps were little more than half as strong due to high local stresses.

3.4.2   Mechanical connections

A variety of mechanical connections (couplers or splices) can be used with the commonly available reinforcing bars. Some can be used only in compression whilst others can be used in tension or compression. Tensile connectors may be threaded or swaged to the reinforcement. A guide to commercially available connections has been prepared by Paterson and Ravenshill (1982). Examples are illustrated in Figure 3.13.

Mechanical connections are useful in congested situations where lapping is not possible or would unduly impede the compaction of concrete. They also have an application where construction is in stages and it is necessary to connect new to existing reinforcement.

Figure 3.13(a) shows a coupler with parallel rolled threads and static strength exceeding the yield strength of the continuous bar, though less than its ultimate strength. This type of connection has survived several million cycles at about half the yield strength of the bar.

Figure 3.13(b) illustrates a metal sleeve swaged onto the ends of the deformed bars to effect continuity. Static and endurance tests up to 4 million cycles showed strengths comparable to the parent bar and fractures clear of the splice.

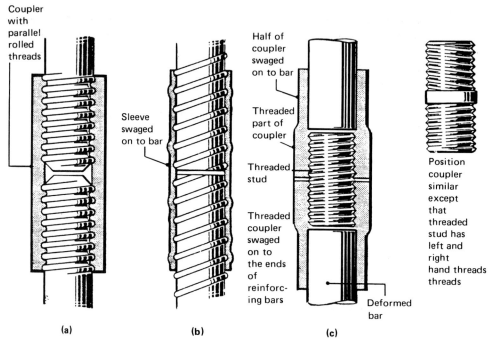

Fig. 3.13
Reinforcement couplers
(Paterson and Ravenshill, 1982, CIRIA)

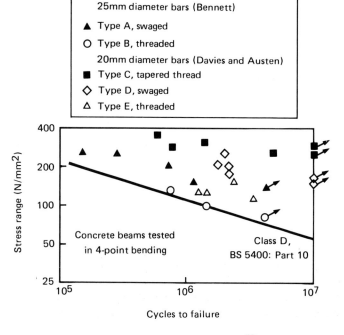

Fig. 3.14
Performance of mechanically
connected Torbar
(Bennett, 1982, Davies and
Austen, 1987, CEB Bulletin
No.188)

58

Figure 3.13(c) shows a threaded coupler comprising internally threaded sleeves swaged onto the two ends of the bars to be joined. The joining stud can have a single thread or, where the bars cannot be rotated, left and right hand with a turnbuckle fitting. Static strengths can be comparable with the parent bar and satisfactory performance has been obtained under repeated loading to 4 million cycles.

Because interaction with the concrete is important, the fatigue strength of a connection is preferably assessed by incorporating it at midspan in the single bar reinforcement of a concrete beam specimen in a bending test. Data for five commercial connections designated A to E are plotted in Figure 3.14.

Types A and B were on 25mm bars tested by Bennett (1982) and Types C to E were on 20mm bars tested by Davies and Austen (1987). Fractures were in the bars near their entry to the connection. The fatigue strength of Types C and D were comparable to continuous bars. The others were not so good but better than Class D of BS5400: Part 10, $(\sigma_r)^3 N = 1.52 \times 10^{12}$, which can be taken as a minimum requirement.

3.4.3   Welding

Both cross welds and butt welds reduce the fatigue strength of steel reinforcing bars. Axial tests on different types of butt welded joints gave fatigue strengths at 2 million cycles about 40 per cent less than that of the continuous bar. Pasko (1973) tested American Grade 60 bars axially and found that welded joints had lives about half those of plain bars. Bannister (1975) tested continuous and welded Torbar in reinforced concrete beams and found a much smaller effect as shown in Figure 3.15.

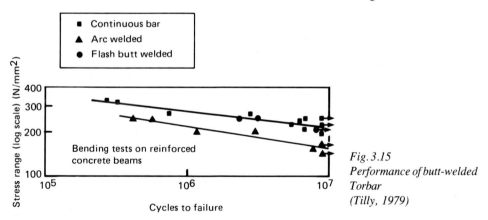

Fig. 3.15
Performance of butt-welded
Torbar
(Tilly, 1979)

This shows that flash butt welded joints behaved as well as continuous bar whilst the arc welded joints had fatigue strengths 15 per cent lower than plain bar at 2 million cycles. Bannister observed that the fatigue curves for the plain and welded bars converge at the yield stress. Soretz (1972) found that butt welded Torbar in concrete beams had fatigue strength 20 to 28 per cent lower than the unwelded bar although his later work showed no reduction. Kokubu and Okamura (1969) tested beams reinforced with bars having pressure welded joints. High strength bars with 600 N/mm² yield stress showed about 20 per cent reduction but intermediate strength bars showed no loss compared with unwelded bar. Bars with 60°arc welds showed 55 per cent reduction.

Burton and Hognestad (1967) tested beams in which stirrups were tack welded, reducing endurances by 28 to 50 per cent in the range 1 million cycles to 5 million cycles. Tests on Unisteel 410 with tack welds showed a reduction of 35 per cent at 2 million cycles.

From the above it can be concluded that welded joints reduce fatigue strength more in axial tests than in bending tests. Where the fatigue strength of reinforced beams was apparently unaffected by welding, it may be that maximum stress initiated cracking at a rib or other stress raiser which did not coincide with a weld. Butt welded joints have a smoother surface profile than the ribs.

Moss investigated the effect of welding in axial tests (1980) and in bending tests (1982). Great care was taken in the preparation and welding procedure following recommendations by the Welding Institute as shown in Figure 3.16.

After preparation, the ends were held in correct alignment in a jig and welded by the manual metal arc process using basic coated low hydrogen electrodes. Typical strength of the weld metal was 463 N/mm² yield stress and 510 N/mm² ultimate. All specimens, axial and bending, failed at the weld and Figure 3.17 shows the typical failure mode of the majority. The results are plotted in Figure 3.18.

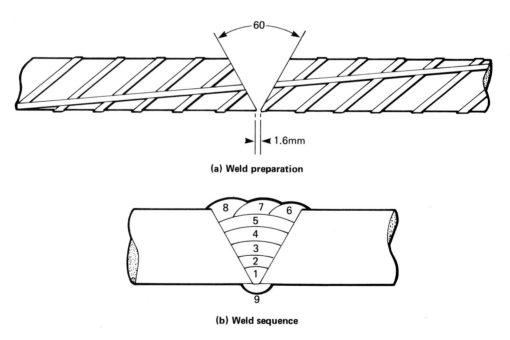

(a) Weld preparation

(b) Weld sequence

Fig. 3.16
Weld preparation and welding sequence
(Moss, 1980, SR 622)

60

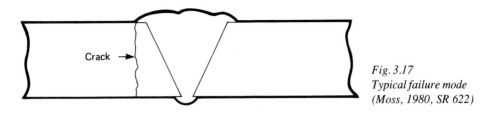

Fig. 3.17
Typical failure mode
(Moss, 1980, SR 622)

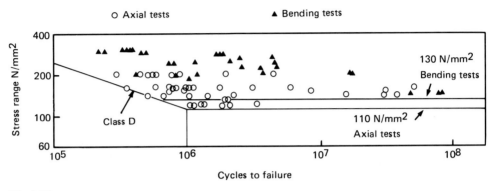

Fig. 3.18
Performance of butt-welded bars
(Tilly and Moss, 1982)

The axial tests showed a reduction in fatigue strength at 10 million cycles of about 40 per cent compared with continuous bars whilst the bending tests showed only about 20 per cent reduction. Class D of BS5400: Part 10 defines a good lower bound to the results for endurances up to 1 million cycles beyond which a fatigue limit of about 110 N/mm² may be construed from the axial tests and about 130 N/mm² from the bending tests.

Hambly (1989) made a study of the effects of tack welding. Good quality tack welds can be advantageous in making reinforcement cages more rigid and therefore more resistant to displacement during concreting and, especially, to the loss of cover. However tack welds do reduce the fatigue strength of reinforcement and the following restrictions are proposed:

1   Tack welds should be either cruciform or lap joints as illustrated in Figure 3.19(a) and (b) respectively.

2   Tack welds should not be used for:

cruciform joints of bars 8 mm or less in diameter unless the Palmgren-Miner summation, w, is less than 0.1

bars stressed primarily by concentrated wheel loads.

steel with carbon content exceeding 0.30 per cent or a carbon equivalent exceeding 0.42 per cent.

61

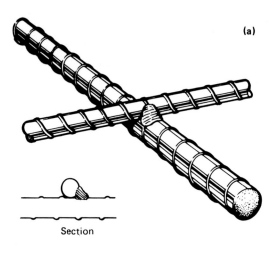

(a)

Section

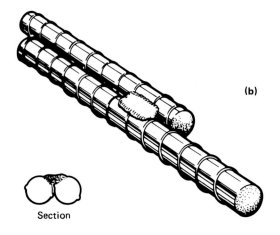

(b)

Section

Fig. 3.19
Forms of tack weld (a)
cruciform and (b) lap joint
(Hambly, 1989)

3   Tack welding should comply with the requirements of BS 7123, Specification for metal arc welding of steel for concrete reinforcement, using mild steel electrodes, hydrogen controlled, or MIG/MAG welding. Undercut should not exceed 5 per cent of diameter.

4   Where the principal tensile stress in the surrounding concrete exceeds $0.24(f_c)^{0.5}$ the fatigue damage to the reinforcement should be checked for Class D of BS5400: Part 10; $(\sigma_r)^3 N = 1.52 \times 10^{12}; \omega < 1$.

5   Bars may be tack welded at bends but not bent after tack welding.

3.5   Corroded bars

Corrosion of steel reinforcement in concrete structures can be caused by the ingress of chlorides such as the deicing salt applied to roads or marine exposure or calcium

62

chloride accelerator in the concrete mix. It may not be feasible to replace damaged bars and it may be necessary to assess their remnant strength. To do this S-N curves for corroded reinforcement are required.Two types of corrosion, general and local, have been described by Cavalier and Vassie (1981).

General corrosion may cover the whole surface of the steel more or less uniformly with comparatively little loss of cross section. It has the familiar red colour of steel exposed to the environment. It is expansive and, if the process continues long enough, it results in cracking and spalling of the concrete cover.

Local corrosion develops at discrete sites on the reinforcement and can result in deep pits; losses of cross section as much as 50 per cent have been reported. The pits are notches causing stress concentrations. The corrosion product is black changing to red if exposed to the atmosphere. It is less expansive and does not disrupt the surrounding concrete, which may be difficult to remove.

Local corrosion is therefore more threatening and more difficult to detect than general corrosion.

Tilly (1988) reported high yield bars with general corrosion but no apparent loss of fatigue performance compared with "as received" material typified by the R1 design curve (See 3.2.6) as shown in Figure 3.20(a).

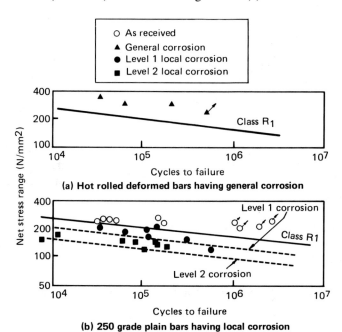

(a) Hot rolled deformed bars having general corrosion

(b) 250 grade plain bars having local corrosion

Fig. 3.20
Performance of 16 mm
corroded reinforcing bars
(Tilly, 1988, CEB Bulletin
No. 188)

However general corrosion which continues long enough results in some loss of cross section and therefore some loss of performance. Figure 3.20(b) illustrates the result of local corrosion of Grade 250 steel after 20 years service in a bridge deck. The loss of fatigue strength is more than can be accounted for by loss of cross section or secondary bending. The data have been arbitrarily divided into two levels of corrosion:

Level 1 pitting with up to 25 per cent loss of section, and

Level 2 pitting with more than 25 per cent loss of section.

Reduction factors for fatigue strength, defined as stress range, are:

1.35 for Level 1 and 1.7 for Level 2.

S-N lines for Levels 1 and 2 are plotted on Figure 3.20(b).

"As received" Grade 250 bars perform better than R1 and are compatible with Grade 460 bars.

Booth *et al.*(1986) reported an investigation of the performance of Torbar immersed in sea water. 32mm bars were fatigue tested in 4-point bending at loading frequencies of 0.1 Hz and 3 Hz. The tests at 0.1 Hz, a typical wave frequency, gave significantly reduced endurances compared with results of the tests at 3 Hz up to 10 million cycles. This can be explained by the fact that more corrosion can occur during the greater time taken for the same number of cycles. Regression analysis of the results of the tests at 0.1 Hz led to a recommended design curve:

$$(\sigma_r)^{2.8} \, N = 1.1 \times 10^{12}$$

The curve is shown with test data in Figure 3.21.

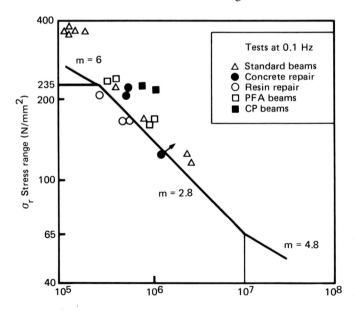

Fig. 3.21
CiO design curve for straight bars in splash zone
(Booth et al., 1986, CEB Bulletin No. 188)

It was considered prudent to modify the exponent to 6 for stress ranges higher than 235 N/mm^2 to accord with the performance of beams tested in air. For more than 10 million cycles the exponent is 4.8 to take account of crack blocking. Other research has shown that there is not much difference in the fatigue performance of different types of steel and that smaller bars behave better than larger ones. Therefore it is reasonable to apply this equation more generally. The complete curve applies to straight bars in the splash zone and is given by the following equations:

$$\text{Log } \sigma_r = 3.27 - (\text{Log } N)/6 \text{ for } \sigma_r \text{ higher than 235 N/mm}^2$$

$$\text{Log } \sigma_r = 4.30 - (\text{Log } N)/2.8 \text{ for } \sigma_r \text{ from 235 to 65 N/mm}^2$$

$$\text{Log } \sigma_r = 3.26 - (\text{Log } N)/4.8 \text{ for } \sigma_r \text{ lower than 65 N/mm}^2.$$

3.6 Summary

Mild steel reinforcement can be plain round or deformed bar.

High yield bars may be:

    hot rolled alloy steel,

    cold twisted or cold drawn mild steel or

    hardened and tempered steel.

Axial fatigue tests can be run at relatively high frequency but great care must be taken with the alignment and gripping of specimens.

Bending fatigue tests simulate service conditions but frequency must be limited to about 3 Hz.

Surface deformations improve bond but reduce fatigue strength. Fatigue strength decreases with larger sizes

Bending, welding and corrosion reduce fatigue strengths.

The following fatigue classifications have been defined:

    Class R1 $\varnothing$<16mm bars $(\sigma_r)^9 N = 0.75 \times 10^{27}$ or $\text{Log } \sigma_r = 2.99 - (\log N)/9$
    3.2.6 and Figure 3.22.

    Class R2 $\varnothing$>16mm bars $(\sigma_r)^9 N = 0.07 \times 10^{27}$ or $\text{Log } \sigma_r = 2.87 - (\log N)/9$
    3.2.6 and Figure 3.23.

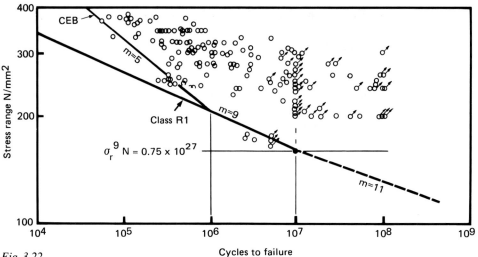

Fig. 3.22
Class R1 in relation to published data
(Tilly, 1988, CEB Bulletin No. 188)

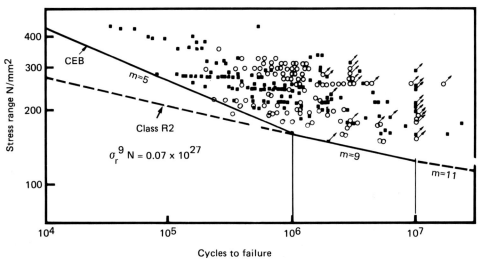

Fig. 3.23
Class R2 in relation to published data
(Tilly, 1988, CEB Bulletin No. 188)

The stress component, m, is modified to 5 for N<1 million and to 11 for N>10 million.

Lapped joints with straight bars have the fatigue strength of continuous bar.

Lapped joints with cranked bars have half the fatigue strength of continuous bar.

66

Class D Connections $(s_r)^3 N = 1.52 \times 10^{12}$ or Log s_r = 4.06 - (log N)/3

Mechanical connections
3.4.2 and Figure 3.13

Butt welded connections have a fatigue limit of 110 N/mm^2 for endurances beyond 1 million cycles
3.4.3 and Figure 3.18.

Torbar Marine splash zone $(\sigma_r)^{2.8} N = 1.1 \times 10^{12}$ 3.5 and Figure 3.21

Reduction factors:

Level 1 corrosion pitting	1.35
Level 2 corrosion pitting	1.7
$25 > D/\emptyset \geq 15$ (slightly bent)	1.3
$15 > D/\emptyset \geq 10$	1.7
$D/\emptyset < 10$ (sharply bent)	3.0

3.7 References

BANNISTER, J L (1969) The behaviour of reinforcing bars under fluctuating stress. Concrete 3, pp405-409.

BANNISTER, J L (1978) Fatigue and corrosion fatigue of Torbar reinforcement. The Structural Engineer, 56A, No. 3 pp82-86.

BANNISTER, J L (1975) Fatigue resistance of reinforcement for concrete. Proc. Conf. Underwater Construction Technology. Department of Civil and Structural Engineering Report. University College, Cardiff.

BENNETT, E W (1982) Fatigue tests of spliced reinforcement in concrete beams. ACI Publication SP-75, pp 177-193.

BOOTH,E D, LEEMING, M B, PATERSON, W S and HODGKIESS, T (1986) Fatigue of reinforced concrete in marine conditions. Marine Concrete 86. International Conference on Concrete in the Marine Environment, pp187-198, London. The Concrete Society.

BURTON,K T and HOGNESTAD, E (1967) Fatigue tests on reinforcing bars - tack welding of stirrups. ACI Journal, Proceedings, v64, pp244-252.

CAVALIER, P G and VASSIE, P R (1981) Investigation and repair of reinforcement corrosion in a bridge deck. Proc. ICE Part 1, 70 pp461-480

DAVIES, M and AUSTIN, M (1987) The fatigue performance of reinforced concrete beams. TRRL Contractor Report CR 53.

FROST, N E, MARSH, K J and POOK, L P (1974) Metal fatigue. pp54-57. Clarendon Press. Oxford.

HAMBLY,E (1989) Study of tack welding of reinforcing steel. TRRL Contractor Report CR 178.

HELGASON, T,HANSON, J M, SOMES, N F, CORLEY, G and HOGNESTAD, E (1969) Fatigue strength of high yield reinforcing bars. NCHRB Report No. 169. Transportation Research Board, Washington.

KOKUBU, M and OKAMURA, H (1969) Fatigue behaviour of high strength deformed bars in reinforced concrete bridges. ACI Publication SP-23, pp301-316.

MOSS, D S (1980) Axial fatigue of high yield reinforcing bars in air. TRRL Report SR622

MOSS, D S (1982) Bending fatigue of high yield reinforcing bars in concrete. TRRL Report SR748

NÜRNBERGER, U (1982) Fatigue resistance of reinforcing steel.Fatigue of Steel and Concrete Structures Colloquium.IABSE, Lausanne. pp229-238.

PASKO, T J (1973) Fatigue of welded reinforcing steel. ACI Journal, Proceedings, v70, pp757-758.

PATERSON, W S and RAVENSHILL, K R (1982) Reinforcement connector and anchorage systems. CIRIA Report No. 92.

SNOWDEN, L C (1971) The static and fatigue performance of concrete beams with high strength deformed bars. Building Research Station CP 7/71.

SORETZ, S (1972) The influence of welds on the fatigue strength of ribbed Torbar. Published by Tor-Isteg Steel Corporation. Luxembourg. Vienna.

TILLY, G P (1979) Fatigue of steel reinforcement bars in concrete: a review. Fatigue of Engineering Materials and Structures. Vol. 2 pp 251-268 Pergamon.

TILLY, G P and MOSS, D S (1982) Long endurance fatigue of steel reinforcement. Fatigue of Steel and Concrete Structures Colloquium IABSE, Lausanne. pp229-238.

TILLY, G P (1988) Durability of concrete bridges. IHT JOURNAL, February.

TRRL (1978) Programme for fatigue testing reinforcement bars. LF 638.

WALKER, E F, AUSTEN, I M, HARRISON,T C and MORLEY, J (1975) Fatigue and corrosion fatigue of reinforcement bars. Proc. Conf. Underwater Construction Technology. Department of Civil and Structural Engineering Report. University College, Cardiff.

WASCHEIDT, H (1965) On the problems of fatigue strength of steel bars embedded in concrete. Dr Ing Thesis, Aachen. Trans. Foreign Literature Study No, 521 PCA Skokie, Illinois.

YANNOPOULOS, P J and EDWARDS, A D (1976) Fatigue characteristics of hot rolled deformed bars. Civil Engineering Department Report CSTR 76/1. Imperial College of Science and Technology, London.

4 Reinforced beams and slabs

4.1 Introduction

In the work mentioned in 3.2 the purpose of concrete beam testing was to investigate the fatigue behaviour of the single reinforcing bar. In Chapters 2 and 3 the fatigue performance of concrete and steel are considered separately. The performance of reinforced concrete depends upon the composite interaction between the steel and the concrete. An under-reinforced member has bending fatigue performance dominated by the steel. Heavily reinforced members which fail in bending and shear are more complicated and bond failures are different.

The concrete is designed to carry compression but, in tensile zones, it does in fact carry various levels of tensile stress up to its ultimate strength, at which point it cracks and tensile force is redistributed to the steel. As fatigue progresses and cracks propagate, the stress distribution changes and fatigue failure is not necessarily by the same mechanism as static failure. The actual stresses in reinforced concrete seldom coincide with stresses calculated using simplified models and this, together with the variability of materials and loads, accounts for the scatter characteristic of fatigue test results.

Prestressed concrete composite beams are considered in Chapter 5.

4.2 Bending failure

The stress gradient in the compression zone provides a reserve for stress to redistribute as the most highly stressed concrete fails under cyclic loading.

Lambotte and Baus (1963) compared over-reinforced beams with uniaxially loaded prisms of the same quality. The load to produce compression fatigue failure of the beams was 70 per cent of their static ultimate load compared with 60 per cent for the prisms. Ople and Hulsbos (1966) simulated the compression zone by eccentically loading concrete prisms. The fatigue strength expressed as the edge stress, computed from the stress-strain curve in static uniaxial compression, increased with eccentricity whilst the total load was not affected. Hence it is on the safe side to use uniaxial compression fatigue data to assess the compression zone of beams.

Tepfers (1973) found that the tensile fatigue strength of high yield deformed bar reinforcement may be as low as 44 per cent of the static yield stress and that Swedish Grades Ks400 Ks600 behave similarly.

It was noted from Figure 3.20(b) that British Grade 250 bars were only marginally inferior to Grade 460 in fatigue performance.

4.3 Shear failure

Design rules seek to ensure that the ultimate limit state will be due to yielding of the main steel rather than a sudden failure of the concrete. Nevertheless Chang and Kesler (1958) have recorded cases of shear fatigue failure although similar beams failed in bending under static loading.

Fatigue of beams without shear reinforcement has been described by Frey and Thürli-mann (1983). The crack pattern developed after the first few cycles and only limited elongation occurred before the critical shear crack appeared. Failure resulted from development of this critical shear crack which crossed the bending cracks. In some beams the main reinforcement separated from the web concrete. Initially deflections and strains increased markedly but the increases reduced with cycling. After the formation of the critical shear crack it is not possible to predict with any confidence the number of cycles to failure.

The shear fatigue strength of beams without shear reinforcement is compared with the bending tension fatigue strength of plain concrete in Figure 4.1.

The shear values lie in and below the lower part of the scatter band of the tension values possibly because the beam develops arching action after the formation of the critical crack.

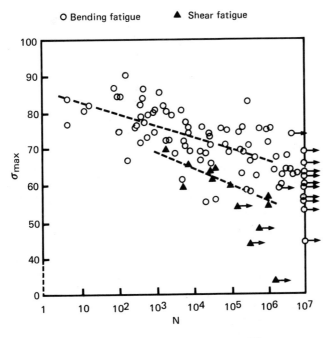

Fig. 4.1
Bending fatigue and shear fatigue
(Kesler, 1953, and Westerberg, 1973, CEB Bulletin No.188)

71

Failure modes for beams with and without stirrups were given by RILEM (1984) as shown in Figure 4.2.

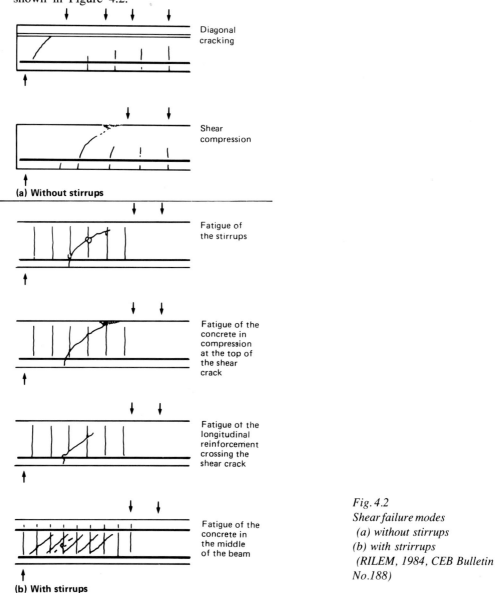

(a) Without stirrups

(b) With stirrups

Fig. 4.2
Shear failure modes
(a) without stirrups
(b) with strirrups
(RILEM, 1984, CEB Bulletin
No.188)

The behaviour of beams with shear reinforcement is affected by the following:

1   the stress history of the stirrups

2   the fact that failure can occur at their lower bends

3   skew cracks in the concrete crossing the stirrups.

Westerberg (1973) tested beams with and without stirrups, each with shear failures and bending failures. The lower test values were for bending failure of main tensile reinforcement.

Frey and Thürlimann (1983) reported tests on beams with shear reinforcement of TOR 50. They recorded local peaks in concrete and steel strains whilst the strain range showed a more regular variation. This suggested a change in load carrying behaviour. Greater web thickness led to reduced strain in the stirrups. The variation in strain in the longitudinal reinforcement clearly confirmed truss action. Out of 74 fatigue breaks only 2 were at the lower bends. The great majority were near the intersections of transverse and longitudinal ribs. No beams failed suddenly in fatigue. The results are plotted in Figure 4.3 together with those of Tepfers (1973).

The fatigue life of the reinforcement appears to be much the same whether it is tensile reinforcement or stirrups.

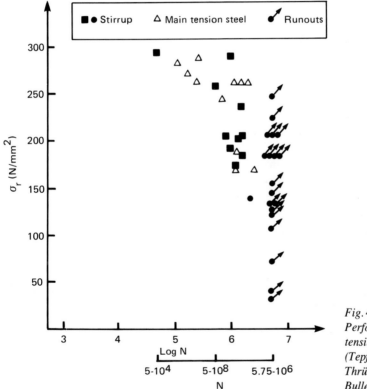

Fig. 4.3
Performance of stirrups and tensile moment reinforcement (Tepfers, 1973, Frey and Thrülimann, 1983, CEB Bulletin No.188)

4.4 Bond failure

If the bond strength between the bar and the concrete is high enough, failure will be in the surrounding concrete where the principal tensile stress exceeds the concrete splitting strength. This type of fatigue is characterised by redistribution of stresses such

73

that it takes more cycles to build up to the failure condition than at this stress level constantly throughout. This is the usual type of failure for deformed bars with normal concrete cover.

If the splitting strength of the surrounding concrete is high enough failure will be along the perimeter of the bar. Pull-out tests have shown that bond fatigue follows the same trends as uniaxial compression or tension fatigue.

In either case the bond stress is not constant along the bar and failure may be of the "zipper" variety.

4.5   Testing beams and slabs

4.5.1   General

A certain amount of research has been done to investigate various other aspects of the fatigue performance of beams and slabs as composite structural members.

4.5.2   Longitudinal shear

Mainstone and Menzies (1967) carried out a number of tests on composite beams of 4.87m span which modelled one type of highway bridge deck. The reinforced concrete slabs were 150mm thick and 600mm wide and the beams were rolled steel joists as shown in Figure 4.4.

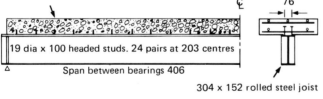

Slab 152 x 304

19 dia x 100 headed studs. 24 pairs at 203 centres

Span between bearings 406

304 x 152 rolled steel joist

Dimensions in mm

Fig. 4.4
Test beam for stud shear connectors
(Mainstone and Menzies, 1967)

The top flanges of the joists were greased and shear transfer was by three types of connector. 4-point loading at about 40 Hz gave constant shear on the outer thirds and zero shear at the centre. Testing with stress ratio 0.1 was carried out by loading the third points in phase. A moving load simulation was achieved by alternating the loading between the third points with a 180° phase difference. This gave stress ratio -1.0, reversed shear in the centre part and unidirectional shear stress ratio 0.5 in the outer thirds. The beam tests for R = 0.1 and 0.5 correlatd well with push out tests for stud, channel and bar connectors. For the reversed loading with R = -1.0 the stud connectors correlated but the channel and bar connectors gave longer lives in the beam tests than in the push outs.

74

Longitudinal shear in composite beams is considered further in 4.7.

4.5.3   Slabs

Matsui *et al.*(1986) tested reinforced concrete slabs to simulate the fatigue problem in bridge decks with a test rig illustrated in Figure 4.5. A single pulsating wheel load in one position gave crack patterns as shown in Figure 4.6(a) which did not accord with the crack pattern, Figure 4.6(b), observed in full scale structures. In later work the slabs 3m long, 2m wide and 190mm thick as shown in Figure 4.5 were loaded with a wheel load of up to 30 tonnes moved 1 metre to and fro by the crank and running to endurances up to 3 million cycles

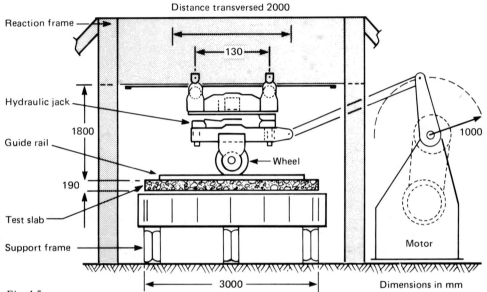

Fig. 4.5
Test rig for bridge deck slab
(Matsui et al.,1986)

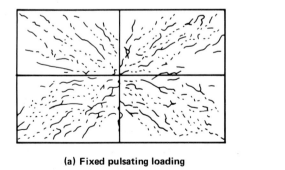

(a) Fixed pulsating loading

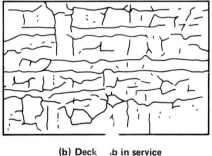

(b) Deck slab in service

Fig. 4.6
Cracking patterns
(Matsui et al.,1986)

4.5.4   Beams in seawater - CiO Report No.19

Hodgkiess, Arthur and Earl (1980,1984,1988) investigated fatigue of reinforced concrete beams in seawater. Each rectangular test beam was 3m long and contained two 10mm diameter Torbars in the top and in the bottom. The 28 day cube strength of the concrete was 60 N/mm^2 and the central 1.17m portion of each beam was enclosed in a waterjacket containing synthetic seawater with a maintained pH of 8. Seawater tests were run at 0.17 Hz and air tests at 0.17 Hz and 3 Hz. The main conclusions for both simple and reverse 4-point bending were as follows.

1   Fatigue failure of reinforcing bars coincided with cracks in the concrete.

2   For the same stress range, endurance was never less in seawater than in air. For stress ranges less than 250 N/mm^2 endurances were up to 16 times longer in seawater than in air probably due to blunting of fatigue cracks in the steel,

3   During fatigue in seawater, but not in air, beam deflections and crack openings decreased significantly due to the deposition of low-solubility salts.

4   Reinforcing bar electrode potentials became very negative in the seawater portion relative to the end portions exposed to the air which were passive.

5   The increased endurances in seawater were accompanied by severe local corrosion. In two tests the cross-section was reduced to 73 and 54 per cent respectively. Pits up to 3 mm deep developed in 2 years.

6   The area of corrosion decreased at lower load amplitudes. Corrosion associated with a concrete crack continued even when the crack width became less than 0.1 mm due to deposits.

7   Large amounts of corrosion products were formed, mostly black magnetite on the bar and becoming brown in the outer regions of the concrete crack.

8   Thus long term performance of reinforced concrete beams may be dictated by local corrosion. This may blunt fatigue cracks in the steel and give long endurance or it may reduce the cross-section to the point of static failure.

Fatigue performance in seawater should not therefore be assumed to be any better than in air.

4.5.5   Beams in seawater - CiO Report No.20

Paterson, Dill and Newby (1981) in Phase I of the Concrete in the Oceans programme carried out comparative fatigue testing of beam specimens in seawater or in air. Each test beam was 3.35m long reinforced with a single Torbar. They drew the following conclusions:

1   Seawater tests showed cyclic stiffening due to formation of brucite (magnesium hydroxide) in the concrete cracks.

2   Crack blocking reduced the stress range.

3   Crack blocking may not necessarily always occur in seawater.

4   Endurances in seawater were significantly lower than in air, especially at low stress range.

5   No endurance limit was established.

6   Simulation of 30m deep seawater made no significant difference to spalling.

7   In seawater, corrosion of the Torbar occurred only at concrete cracks and for 20mm on both sides.

8   Crack blocking tended to stabilise electropotential levels but did not prevent corrosion.

9   Fatigue fractures always coincided with concrete cracks.

10   Fatigue crack propagation was by a striation mechanism and fracture was by ductile shear. For all tests in air and for high stress range tests in seawater, initiation was at rib intersections. For low stress range tests in seawater, initiation was at corrosion sites.

Concrete in the Oceans Phase II research by Paterson and Dill (1988) was concerned with pfa concrete and alternative concrete repair methods. Repair pockets were as detailed in Figure 4.7.

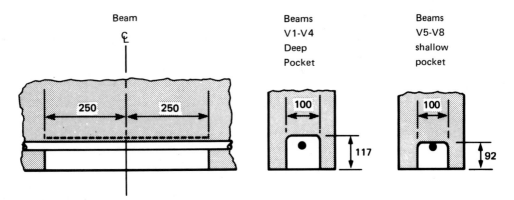

Fig. 4.7
Repair pocket for tests in seawater
(Paterson, Dill and Newby, 1981)

This research led to the following conclusions.

1   Cyclic stiffening was confirmed in beams with 20 per cent replacement of cement with pfa, beams with cementitious and resin repairs and beams with cathodic protection.

2   Endurances for beams in seawater were the same within the general scatter as those of the standard beams tested in sea water and in air in Phase I with one exception. Beams with resin repairs developed a major crack at one end of the repair and had only half the endurance of other beams.

3   Fatigue failure of the Torbar always occurred at cracks in the concrete cover.

4   In the seawater tests fatigue initiation was generally associated with relatively large areas of shallow corrosion.

Separately these test programmes did not provide sufficient data to confirm S-N curves but, combined, they led to the curve shown in Figure 3.21.

4.6 Permanent formwork

Permanent formwork supports freshly placed in situ concrete and is left in place. Therefore it must be compatible with the in situ concrete and be durable in its service environment.

In bridge works in the UK permanent formwork is classified as either structurally participating with the overlying in situ concrete or structurally non-participating as follows:

Structurally non-participating:

Glass reinforced plastic (GRP)

Glass reinforced cement (GRC)

Profiled steel sheet

Structurally participating:

Precast concrete units

To ensure structural participation, precast concrete units must be integrated fully with the in situ concrete. For instance the units could be of inverted T form or have projecting stirrups across the interface. One patented system uses a precast soffit plank as the tension flange in conjunction with reinforcement bars to act as the compression member of a lattice girder to support the wet in situ concrete. The compression bars are located at the correct height above the plank by tack welded triangular stirrups. The fatigue performance of the completed composite slab may be assessed as reinforced concrete taking account of the stress history of all its elements - concrete, bars and welds. As it forms part of the completed structure, it must comply with all of the design and specification requirements for the permanent works.

Structurally non-participating permanent formwork, though not regarded as structurally competent, does in fact suffer strains under service loading conditions. It is therefore necessary to be assured that it can withstand this without disintegrating.

Profiled steel sheet suitably protected is used widely for floor slabs and has given good service in bridge decks although panel edges, especially where site cutting damages the protective treatment, tend to be vulnerable to corrosion.

Fatigue tests by Beales and Ives (1990) on commercially available GRC and GRP permanent formwork were encouraging for GRP but not for the GRC design tested.

GRP test specimens as detailed in Figure 4.8 were supplied by the manufacturer complete with in situ concrete topping. The concrete had 28 day cube strength exceeding 60 N/mm² but was poorly compacted.

The slab was designed to give a stress in the reinforcing bars of 235 N/mm² under a central test load of 100 kN. There were three specimens; No.1 was subjected to a static test to 100 kN, Nos 2 and 3 to 42.5 kN which gave a steel stress of 100 N/mm². The load-deflection curves are shown in Figure 4.9

Each specimen was subjected to 10 million cycles of loading with the maximum load of 42.5 kN. This criterion was based upon the concept of a non-propagating stress range as described in BS 5400: Part 10. Firstly the range was from 20 to 42.5 kN at 3 Hz until cracking had stabilised and then continued at 15 to 42.5 kN and 5 to 7.5 Hz. Although there was some deterioration of the concrete the GRP permanent formwork withstood the 10 million cycles without distress.

Similar tests were conducted by Beales and Ives (1990) on GRC specimens of the design shown in Figure 4.10. In manufacture, great care must be taken to hold the polystyrene fillers accurately in position during spraying of the cement and glass fibres; otherwise thicknesses of the section vary. Excessive cracking and debonding occurred before 10 million cycles. This multi-cell type has suffered fatigue failure in service due to its depth below the structural deck slab.

Asbestos has been used in the past as structurally non-participating permanent formwork but has been superseded. Timber, plywood and chipboard have also been used but their long term durability is uncertain.

(a) End view

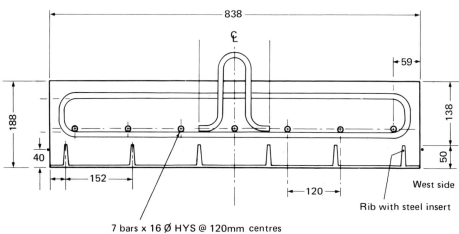

838

Ȼ

59

188

138

40

50

152

120

West side

Rib with steel insert

7 bars x 16 Ø HYS @ 120mm centres

(b) Side view

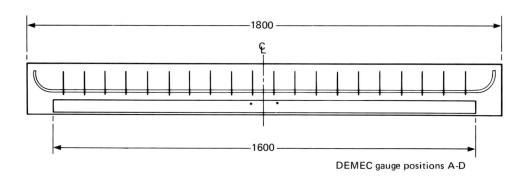

1800

Ȼ

1600

DEMEC gauge positions A-D

Fig. 4.8
GRP test specimen
(Beales and Ives, 1990)

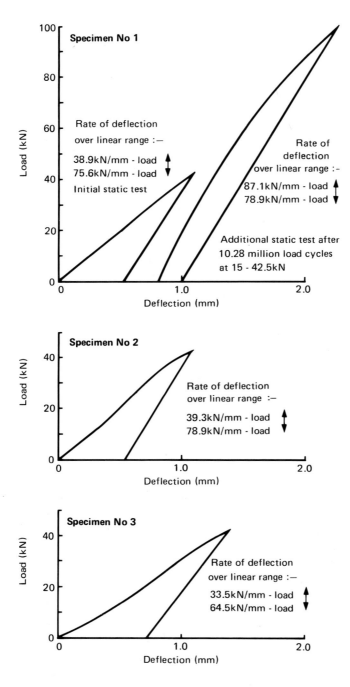

Fig. 4.9
Load-deflection data for GRP specimens
(Beales and Ives, 1990)

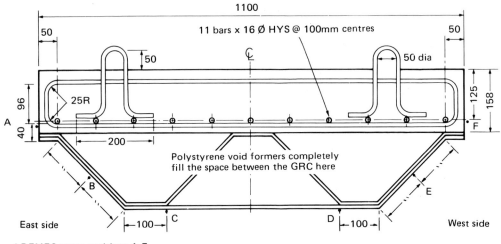

1100

11 bars x 16 Ø HYS @ 100mm centres

50

50

50 dia

℄

25R

96

40

200

125

158

A

F

Polystyrene void formers completely
fill the space between the GRC here

B

E

East side

100

C

D

100

West side

• DEMEC gauge positions A-F

(a) End view

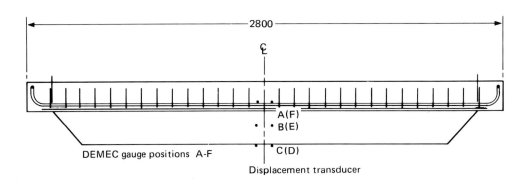

2800

℄

DEMEC gauge positions A-F

A(F)
B(E)
C(D)

Displacement transducer

(b) Side view

Fig. 4.10
GRC test specimen
(Beales and Ives, 1990)

4.7 Longitudinal shear in concrete beams

4.7.1 Introduction

Hughes (1987) reported work done under contract to TRRL to validate the provisions
of BS 5400 for longitudinal shear between precast concrete beams and the in situ
concrete deck slabs of composite bridges. The test work included 83 push-off tests, 47
small beam tests and 16 full-scale composite beam tests.

82

4.7.2 Concrete surface roughness

The first requirement was to define in measurable terms the surface of the precast beam against which the in situ concrete is cast. Table 4.1 gives the roughness of the types of surface used compared with one to represent an internal shear plane, termed monolithic and obtained by measuring the failure surfaces of split cylinders.

TABLE 4.1

Concrete surface roughnesses

Surface	Description	Average roughness (mm)	Coefficient of variation (%)	Characteristic roughness (mm)
Type 0	Monolithic	1.69	24	1.02
Type 1	Roughened	1.24	18	0.87
Type 2	Rough-as-cast	0.72	27	0.40
Type 3	Smoothed	0.16	19	0.11

The variation in roughness involved some overlap between the different surfaces some of which are illustrated in photographs (a) to (f) in Figure 4.11. Surfaces of test specimens were made at the least rough end of the range for each type so that they represent worst cases.

4.7.3 Push-off tests

Details of the push-off test specimens and typical failure modes are shown in Figure 4.12. Composite specimens always failed along the interface. Those with less than a critical area of stirrups failed suddenly when the bond strength was exceeded. Those wih more stirrups failed in a ductile manner as the steel yielded. Cracking stresses are illustrated in Figure 4.13 and ultimate stresses in Figure 4.14. A variant of the Type 2 surface was prepared by spraying a 0.03mm layer of cellulose paint to simulate a pre-existing crack. The cracking stress v_{cr} was of course zero for these specimens.

Characteristic cracking stresses are 3.0, 2.5, 2.0 and 1.5 N/mm^2 regardless of the area of stirrups. Ultimate stresses are equal to the cracking stresses for brittle failures and increase with the area of stirrups for ductile failures.

4.7.4 Small beam tests

37 small beam specimens were cast as shown in Figure 4.15; 5 were monolithic and 5 were fully composite. They were supported on rollers and loaded to failure in 3-point bending with the results shown in Figure 4.16.

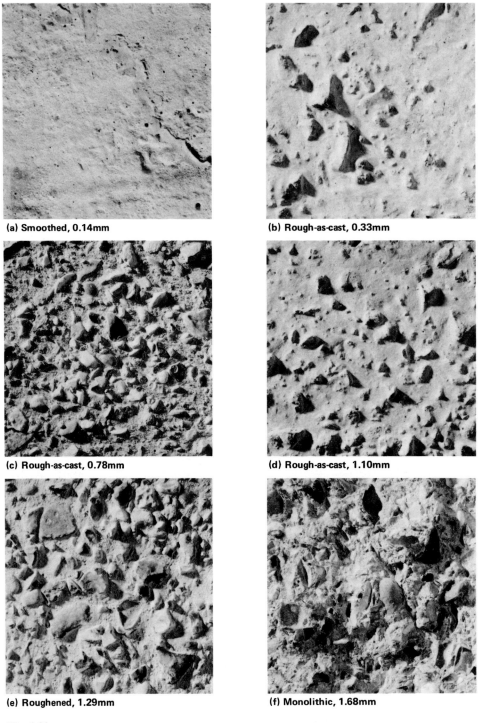

(a) Smoothed, 0.14mm

(b) Rough-as-cast, 0.33mm

(c) Rough-as-cast, 0.78mm

(d) Rough-as-cast, 1.10mm

(e) Roughened, 1.29mm

(f) Monolithic, 1.68mm

Fig. 4.11
Surface types and roughnesses
(Hughes, 1987, TRRL Contractor Report 52)

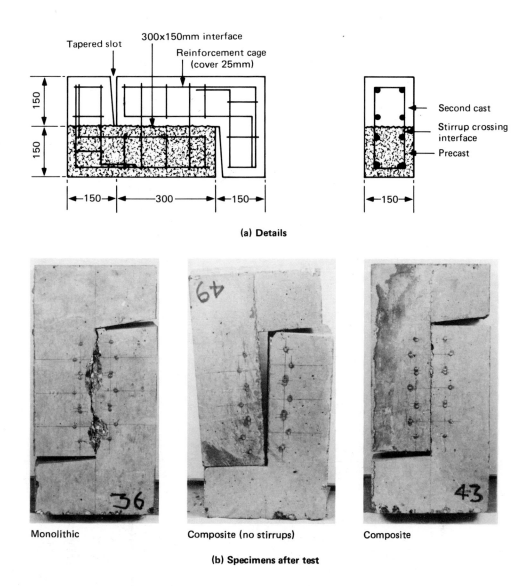

(a) Details

Monolithic | Composite (no stirrups) | Composite

(b) Specimens after test

Fig. 4.12
Push-off specimens
(Hughes, 1987, TRRL Contractor Report 52)

The ultimate stresses in these tests were higher than the push-out stresses due to coexisting compression across the interface in the beam situation. Results of tests with the interface in the tension or compression zone and with different shear spans are given in Figure 4.17.

Interfaces in compression zones were slightly stronger than those in tension zones and interfaces in short shear spans were slightly stronger than those in the longer shear spans. 8 of the small beams were subjected to 1000 repetitions of loading at the same test

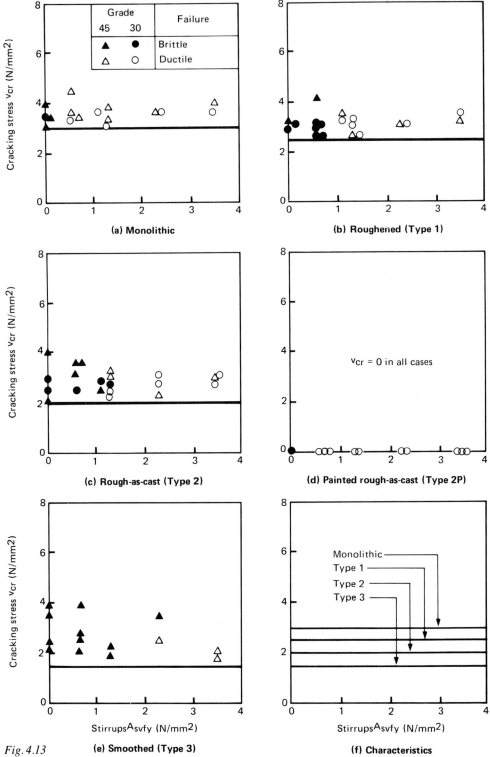

Fig.4.13
Cracking stresses
(Hughes, 1987, TRRL Contractor Report 52)

86

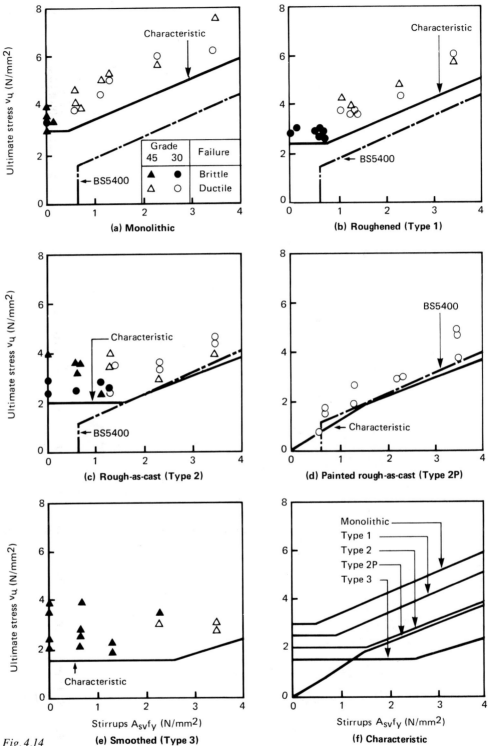

Fig. 4.14
Ultimate stresses
(Hughes, 1987, TRRL Contractor Report 52)

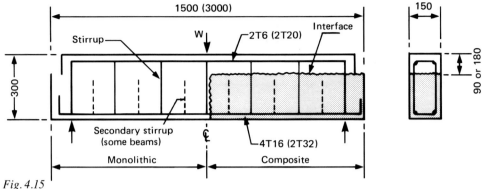

Fig. 4.15
Test beam details
(Hughes, 1987, TRRL Contractor Report 52)

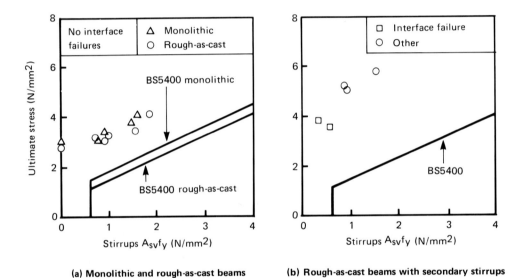

(a) Monolithic and rough-as-cast beams   (b) Rough-as-cast beams with secondary stirrups

Fig. 4.16
Ultimate stresses for (a) monolithic and (b) rough-as-cast beams
(Hughes, 1987, TRRL Contractor Report 52)

level at 0.25 Hz and then loaded to failure. These beams were if anything stronger than those which had only static loading.

4.7.5   Full scale beam tests

16 full scale M3 section bridge beams were subjected to repeated loading tests. M3 section beams are generally used for bridge spans of 18-19m but the 8m long test specimens provided reasonably long shear spans and were suitable for the purpose of investigating longitudinal shear.

88

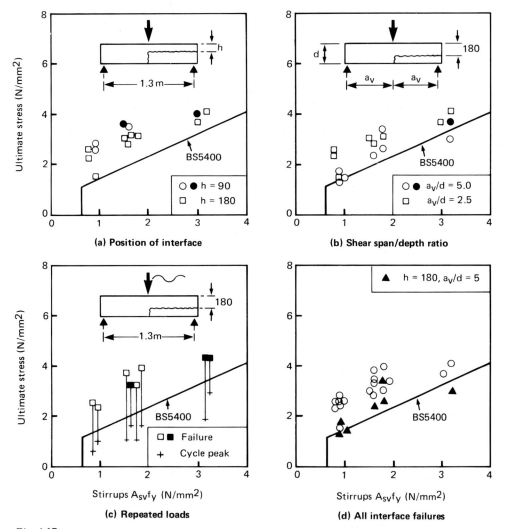

Fig. 4.17
Ultimate stresses for painted rough-as-cast beams
(Hughes, 1987, TRRL Contractor Report 52)

8 beams were cast with the manufacturer's normal rough-as-cast finish. After filling the mould and compaction was complete, the surface was finished with a stiff bristle brush to the correct level with a stippling action. The remaining 8 beams were left as they were after vibration and given no brush treatment. The two surfaces are shown in Figure 4.18 and the test programme in Table 4.2.

The brush stippling did not affect the measured roughness which was on average 1.4mm compared with 0.72mm and 0.79mm for the rough-as-cast surfaces of the push-off specimens and the small beams respectively. The beams were typical of normal production. The 16 beams were in 4 sets having 0.15, 0.38, 0.60 and 0.75 per cent stirrups across the interface.

TABLE 4.2

Finishes to tops of M-beams

Beams	Surface	Support	a_v/b	Test
1,5,9 13	brushed	simple	4.2 3.1	static
2,6,10 14	brushed	simple	4.2 3.1	pre-cracked 0.03, cycled and static
4,8 12,15	rough-as-cast	simple	4.2 3.1	pre-cracked 0.10, cycled and static
3,7,11,16	rough-as-cast	internal	3.1	pre-cracked 0.10, cycled and static

The internal support represents the inner support of a continuous beam with hogging moment. Concrete strengths varied from 64 to 80 N/mm² for the beams and from 36 to 46 N/mm² for the in situ slab. For Beam No.8 the strengths were 72 N/mm² and 44 N/mm². This beam was the only one that failed in longitudinal shear and was therefore reported in fuller detail than the others. The area of stirrups was 0.38 per cent which for the 0.2 per cent proof stress 480 N/mm² gave a longitudinal shear value 1.82 N/mm². The unfactored longitudinal shear strength was taken as 1.25 (0.50 + 0.7x1.82) = 2.2 N/mm². Under test the interface cracked at 2.4 N/mm². Load was increased until the interface stress was 3.7 N/mm² and then released leaving an interface crack width of about 0.1mm. 10000 cycles were then applied with an interface stress range of 0.3 to 2.0 N/mm². This had no significant effect and the beam was then loaded to failure which occurred at an interface stress of 4.5 N/mm². Modes of failure of the other beams varied: flexural, interface shear, web crushing, shear compression or some combination of these. Interface shear contributed to failure in 5 beams in addition to Beam No.8. None of the statically loaded group failed along the interface but 6 (Nos.2,14,4,8,12 and 15) out of the 12 cycled beams did. There were no interface shear failures in the internal support group. Thus cycling seems to weaken the interface to some extent.

4.8 Summary

The fatigue performance of an under-reinforced concrete beam is dominated by the steel. Heavily reinforced members fail in bending or shear depending on whether the concrete or steel strength is critical. Fatigue failure is not necessarily in the same mode as static failure.

The stress gradient in the compression zone of a beam provides a reserve for stress to redistribute as the most highly stressed concrete fails. It is on the safe side to use uniaxial compression fatigue data to assess the compression zone of a beam.

(a) Brushed rough-as-cast

(b) Rough-as-cast

Fig. 4.18
Surfaces of M-beams
(Hughes, 1987, TRRL Contractor Report 52)

The fatigue performance of high yield steel reinforcement is only marginally better than that of mild steel.

Design rules seek to ensure that the ultimate condition is by yielding of steel rather than by sudden failure of the concrete. After the formation of a critical shear crack it is not possible to predict with confidence the number of cycles to failure.

91

The behaviour of stirrups depends upon their stress history and their life is much the same as tensile reinforcement.

Bond failure may be by tensile cracking of the surrounding concrete or, if its splitting strength is high enough, it may be along the perimeter of the bar.

Shear connectors in a composite beam have longer endurances than those indicated by push-out tests.

In seawater, fatigue failure of reinforcing bars generally coincides with cracks in the concrete. Some tests have suggested endurances in seawater longer than in air and some the opposite. Fatigue of reinforcement may be dictated by local corrosion and loss of section to the point of static failure. On the other hand corrosion may be inhibited by crack blocking and fatigue life extended by the blunting of cracks in the steel. The depth of seawater does not seem to make any difference to the process. Resin repairs have half the life of the reinforced concrete in the same environment.

Permanent formwork is treated as either structurally participating (precast concrete) or structurally non-participating (GRP, timber). Structurally participating formwork is included in the design of the permanent work. Non-participating formwork should have adequate fatigue performance to remain serviceable under the stresses induced in service. Tests have shown that a GRP product is promising in this respect.

Longitudinal shear failure surfaces classified as monolithic, roughened, rough-as-cast and smooth had characteristic push-off cracking stresses 3.0, 2.5, 2.0 and 1.5 N/mm^2 respectively regardless of the area of stirrups.

Interfaces in compression zones were slightly stronger than those in tension zones and short shear spans behaved slightly better than long shear spans.

Push-out tests, small beam tests and repeated loading tests on full scale composite beams showed that the design rules in BS 5400: Part 4: 1984 for longitudinal shear are conservative.

4.9   References

ARTHUR, P D, EARL, J C and HODGKIESS, T (1980) Corrosion fatigue in concrete for marine applications. ACI Symposium. Recent research in fatigue of concrete structures. San Juan, Puerto Rico. ACI Special Publication SP-75, pp1-24.

BEALES, C and IVES, D I (1990) Behaviour of permanent formwork. TRRL Report RR254.

CHANG, T S and KESLER, C E (1958) Static and fatigue strength in shear of beams with tensile reinforcement. ACI Journal pp1033-1058.

FREY, R and THÜRLIMANN, B (1983) Ermüdungsversuche an Stahlbetonbalken mit und ohne Schubbewehrung. Institut für Baustatik und Konstruktion, ETH, Bericht Nr 7801-1. Zürich. p166.

HODGKIESS, T, ARTHUR, P D and EARL, J C (1984) Corrosion fatigue of reinforced concrete in seawater. Materials Performance Vol. 23(7), pp27-31.

HODGKIESS, T and ARTHUR, P D (1988) Fatigue and corrosion effects in reinforced concrete beams partially submerged in seawater and subjected to reverse bending. Concrete in the Oceans Technical Report No. 19.

HUGHES, G (1987) Longitudinal shear in composite concrete bridge beams. Part 2: Experimental investigation and recommendations. TRRL Contractor Report 52.

LAMBOTTE, H and BAUS, R (1963) Étude expérimentale de l'effet de la fatigue sur le component de poutres en béton armé. Revue C, Nos. 3 and 4.

MAINSTONE, R J and MENZIES, J B (1967) Shear connectors in steel-concrete composite beams for bridges. Part 2. Fatigue tests on beams. J.Concrete 1(10) pp351-358

MATSUI, S, SONADA, K, OKAMURA, H and OKADA, K (1986) Concepts for the deterioration of highway bridge decks and fatigue studies. International Symposium. Fundamental theory of reinforced and prestressed concrete. Nanjing, China, Vol. 2 pp831-838.

OPLE, F S and HULSBOS, C L (1966) Probable fatigue life of plain concrete with stress gradient. ACI Journal, Proceedings, vol. 63, No. 1, pp59-82.

PATERSON, W S, DILL, M J and NEWBY, R (1981) Fatigue strength of reinforced concrete in seawater. Concrete in the Oceans Technical Report No. 7.

PATERSON, W S and DILL, M J (1988) Fatigue strength of reinforced concrete in seawater-Results from Phase II. Concrete in the Oceans Technical Report No. 20.

PRICE, W I J, HAMBLY, E C and TRICKLEBANK, A H (1989) Review of fatigue in concrete marine structures. Concrete in the Oceans Technical Report No. 12.

RILEM Committee 36-RDL Long term random dynamic loading of concrete structures Materiaux et constructions. Essais et recherches. No. 87, pp1-28.

TEPFERS, R (1973) A theory of bond applied to overlapped tensile reinforcement splices for deformed bars. Chalmers Tekniska Hogskola, Instituten for Betongbyggnad, Publication 73: 2, Goteborg, p328.

WESTERBERG, B (1973) Utmattningsförsök på armerade betongbalkar. Fatigue tests of reinforced concrete beams. Royal Institute of Technology, Department of Structural Engineering and Bridge Building. Publication 73:1. Stockholm.

5 Prestressed beams

5.1 Prestressing steel

5.1.1 Introduction

Fatigue of prestressing steel has not in the past been considered to be a problem. In fully prestressed members, in which there is no cracking, the maximum stress range in the steel is α_e times the sum of the precompression and the tensile strength of the concrete at the level of the steel, where α_e is the modular ratio. This is in the order of 50 to 100 N/mm^2 and well below the fatigue strengths of available tendon material at 2 million cycles which are typically as given in Table 5.1. It was estimated that structures do not have more than 2 million repetitions of their maximum design load in their service lifetime and this became the arbitrary number of cycles for specifying fatigue performance. However it is now understood that low stress cycles do contribute to fatigue damage. Interest in fatigue has been sharpened with the advent of partial prestressing and also the need to assess older prestressed structures which may have suffered deterioration from other causes.

TABLE 5.1 *

Typical fatigue strengths of prestressing steels

FeP,type,surface geometry	$\varnothing$ (mm)	Fatigue strength at 2 million cycles (N/mm^2)	
		$\sigma_{max} = 0.55 f_{pk}$	$\sigma_{max} = 0.9 f_{0.2}$
Hot rolled smooth	26-36	290-380	230-325
835/1030 threaded	25-36	235-240	210-220
Heat treated smooth	6.0-14	335-340	240-295
1420/1570 ribbed	5.2-14	295	230
Cold drawn smooth	5.0-12.2	290-585	200-430
1479/1670 profiled	5.0-7.5	230-400	210-310
1570/1770 7-wire strand	9.3-15.3	220-290	205-250

* Based on Table 4.3 from CEB Bulletin No.188

5.1.2 Types of tendon

Steels used for prestressing tendons contain rather less than 1 per cent of carbon; their high strength and ductility are achieved by various combinations of alloying refinements, heat treatment and cold working. There are three forms:

1   Alloy bar

2   Strand

3   Cold drawn wire

The various manufacturing processes have been described by Longbottom (1973).

Wire or strand is used for pre-tensioning.

Wire, strand or alloy bar is used for post-tensioning.

Andrew and Turner (1985) have described the various post-tensioning systems used in the United Kingdom.

The CEB-FIP Model Code (1990) requires prestressing steels to be designated FeP followed by the nominal tensile strength range in N/mm^2, eg FeP 1570/1770.

5.1.3 Fatigue strength

Fatigue performance of prestressing steels is customarily quoted as the stress range in constant amplitude tests for 2 million cycles with a specified maximum stress. This stress range is quite widely referred to as the endurance limit although it has not been proved to be such. It is the usual acceptance criterion and typical values are given in Table 5.1

The Smith diagrams due to Nürnberger (1981) in Figure 5.1 illustrate the decrease in range at higher mean stress levels. Baus and Brenneisen (1968) show the derivation of Smith diagrams from the stress ranges at 2 million cycles taken from three Wöhler curves as shown in Figure 5.2.

Calderale and Corona (1962) reported that the influence of cycling frequency was to increase fatigue strength. Figure 5.3 shows their results and Figure 5.4 shows the effect of fretting investigated by Endo, Goto and Nakamura (1969), whereby fretting lowers, fatigue strength but the influence of frequency is the same as for no fretting.

The regression line for fatigue of prestressing strand in Figure 5.5 was derived by Paulson, Frank and Breen (1983) from the results of the following: Warner and Hulsbos (1966), Tide and Van Horn (1966), Edwards and Picard (1972) and Cullimore (1972). It represents 97.3 per cent probability of survival at the 95 per cent confidence level and

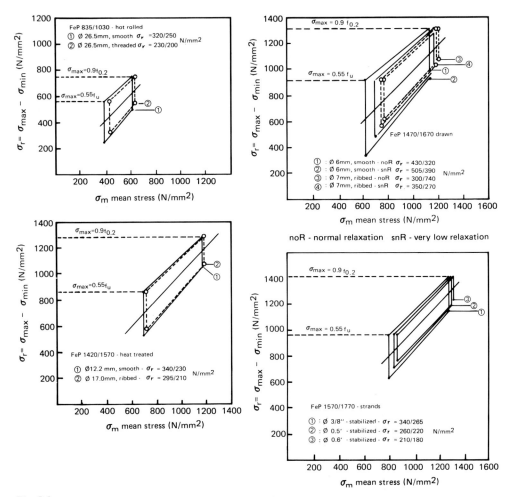

Fig. 5.1
Smith diagrams for prestressing steels
(Nürnberger, 1981, CEB Bulletin No.188)

extrapolates to a value of about 100 N/mm² at 10 million cycles. The exponent is about 3.9 but data is rather sparse over about 1 million cycles. For longer endurances there may be fatigue limits as claimed by Canteli, Esslinger and Thürlimann (1984) from the results of tests on 9.3, 12.7 and 15.3 mm diameter strand. They lacked shorter-life data but the considerable amount of data around 1 million cycles strongly suggests a flattening of the curve. A satisfactory lower bound, almost coincident with the line proposed by Paulson, Frank and Breen (1983), is provided by 200 N/mm² at 1 million cycles with a stress exponent of 4 as shown on Figure 5.5.

Figure 5.6 due to Nürnberger (1981) shows the relative fatigue performance of different types of prestressing bars. It is clear that smooth bars perform better than ribbed bars but it is not possible to give generalized performances for the latter because their geometry tends to be peculiar to each manufacturer.

96

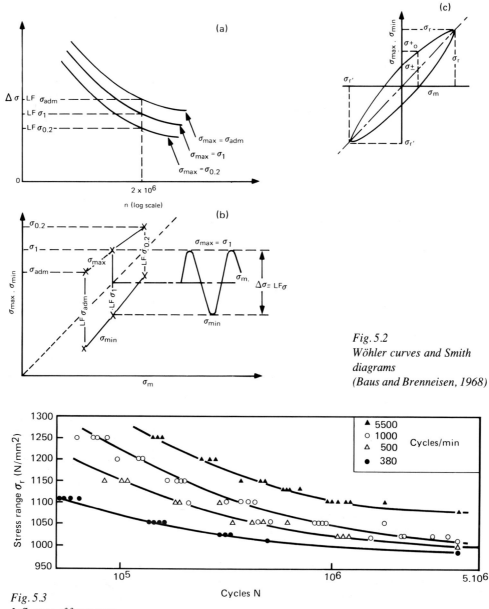

Fig. 5.2
Wöhler curves and Smith
diagrams
(Baus and Brenneisen, 1968)

Fig. 5.3
Influence of frequency
(Calderale and Corona, 1962, CEB Bulletin No.188)

In Figure 5.4 the effect of fretting was noted in the context of the frequency of load cycling. Fretting can occur between tendon and duct in partially prestressed members, in bare tendons or tendons in voided ducts. The main parameters of fretting corrosion are slip and transverse pressure. These were investigated by Funk (1969) with the rather generalized test device shown in Figure 5.7 which yielded the results plotted in Figure 5.8.

97

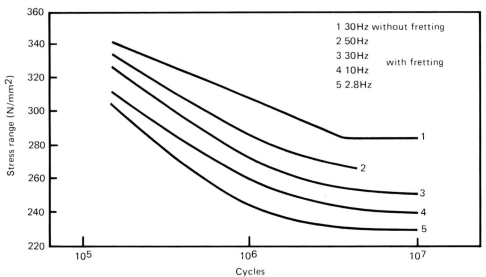

Fig. 5.4
Fretting at different frequencies
(Endo, Goto and Nakamura, 1969, CEB Bulletin No.188)

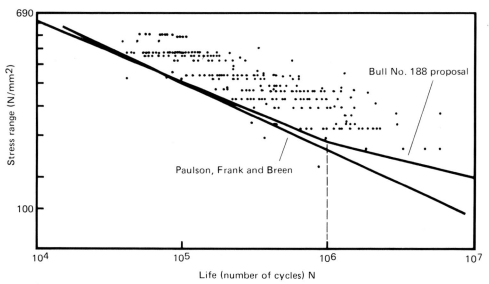

Fig. 5.5
Design models for strand
(Paulson, Frank and Breen, 1983, CEB Bulletin No.188)

It can be seen that transverse pressure reduces endurances but the effect is less at high pressures. The amount of slip has a similar effect. Funk showed flattening of the curves after about 1 million repetitions in the control tests without fretting but, by contrast, in the fretting tests, no flattening at 10 million cycles.

As with reinforcing bars, corrosion adversely affects the fatigue performance of prestressing steel. Engineers, being aware of the potentially serious consequences of

98

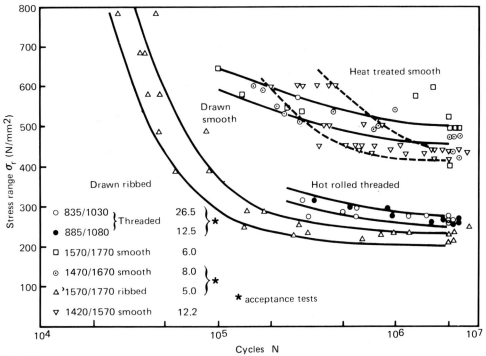

Fig. 5.6
S-N curves for various bars and wires
(Nürnberger, 1981, CEB Bulletin No.188)

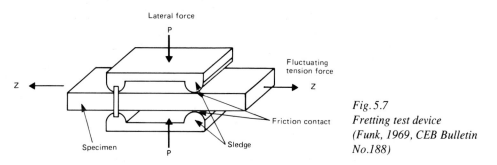

Fig. 5.7
Fretting test device
(Funk, 1969, CEB Bulletin
No.188)

corrosion damage to tendons, take great care to protect them. The durability of pre-tensioning tendons does not seem to be in question and post-tensioning tendons are usually protected by carefully regulated pressure grouting with cement grout. Despite the utmost care however, ducts may not always be completely filled and, although Woodward (1981) has reported that the presence of even some grout in the duct provides an environment in which corrosion does not take place, the intended protection may not continue indefinitely.

As with reinforcing steel, the worst form of corrosion is pitting. Neubert and Nürnberger (1983) investigated the effect of pitting on the fatigue strength of smooth high yield bar and presented the results shown in Figure 5.9.

99

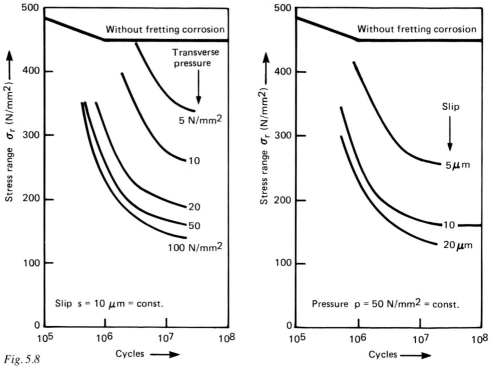

Fig. 5.8
Effect of transverse pressure and slip
(Funk, 1969, CEB Bulletin No.188)

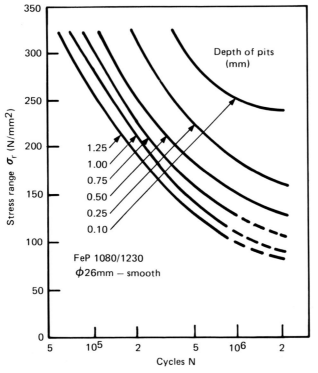

Fig. 5.9
S-N curves for corroded
prestressing steel
(Neubert and Nürnberger,
1981, CEB Bulletin No.188)

Erdmann, Kordina and Neisecke (1982) analysed the effect of corrosion on prestressing steel removed from demolished structures. Corrosion was found in incompletely filled ducts and in voids at anchorages but, as also reported by Woodward (1981) damage was slight provided moisture was excluded and the depth of pits was mostly between 20 and 30 μm. Pits of 50 μm adversely affected fatigue strength and pits from 150 to 250 μm caused reductions as much as 50 per cent. No direct relationship could be established but it was noted that deep pits in small wires resulted in some failures but this seldom occurred in large diameter bars. Typical reduction in fatigue strength of 5.2 mm

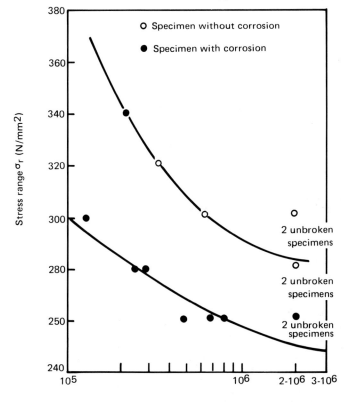

Fig. 5.10
Corroded prestressing steel
FeP 1420/1520 5.2 mm
(Erdmann, Kordina and
Neisecke, 1982, CEB Bulletin
No.188)

Tilly (1988) has reported fatigue tests up to 10 million cycles carried out at TRRL on strand of British origin. The results of the tests on pristine and lightly corroded strand were very similar to those of Paulson, Frank and Breen and led to the same lower bound as shown in Figure 5.5. The performance of severely corroded strand recovered from the demolition of structures 16 to 21 years old fell about two standard deviations lower, corresponding to a reduction factor of 1.35, as shown in Figure 5.11.

The fatigue behaviour of prestressing tendons in grouted ducts has been investigated by several workers by testing partially prestressed beams.

Rigon and Thürlimann (1988) at ETH, Zürich, tested 15 T-beams 6.7 m long as shown in Figure 5.12.

They found that curved cables in the concrete beam had significantly lower fatigue

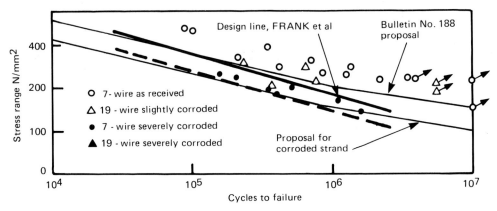

(strands removed from structures after 16–21 years)

Fig. 5.11
Fatigue performance of corroded prestressing strand
(Tilly, Durability of concrete bridges. IHT Journal, Feb. 1988)

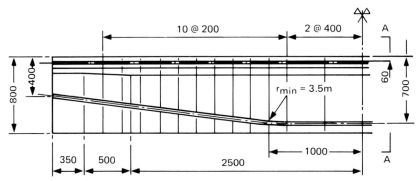

Fig. 5.12
T-beams tested at ETH, Zürich
(Rigon and Thürlimann, 1988, CEB Bulletin No.188)

strengths than similar bare cables. Plastic ducts were better than steel ducts in this respect.

Müller (1985) at TU Munich carried out similar tests using 3m beam specimens with the results in Figure 5.13.

The fatigue strengths of tendons in the beams were 40 to 70 per cent lower than those of straight tendons in air.

Cordes and Trost (1984) at RWTH, Aachen, tested straight specimens, made from the same melt as those tested at Munich, in a device which simulated ducting by the application of transverse pressure as shown with the results in Figure 5.14.

It will be noticed that the various fatigue strengths at 2 million cycles are shown as endurance limits. The values are given in Table 5.2.

TABLE 5.2

Munich and Aachen test results

FeP,type & geometry		Fatigue strengths at 2 million cycles $\sigma_{MAX} = 0.55 f_{pk}$		Reduction factor due to fretting
		Without fretting N/mm^2	With fretting N/mm^2	
1080/1230	hot rolled ribbed Ø 26.5 mm	285	M 200 A -	0.70
1420/1570	heat treated smooth Ø 12.2 mm	390	M 175 A 170	0.44
1470/1670	cold drawn smooth Ø 7.0 mm	350	M - A 160	0.46
1570/1770	strands Ø 15.3 mm	250	M 150 A 170	0.64

Kordina and Gunther (1982), working at Braunschweig, tested different tendon splicing systems using 5.6m beams loaded by 4-point bending. Particulars of the tendons are given in Table 5.3.

Using the Braunschweig results plotted in Figure 5.15 König and Gerhardt (1986) derived the regression line with a nominal fatigue strength at 2 million cycles of 65 N/mm^2 stress range compared with published fatigue strengths of 98, 78, 98 and 90 N/mm^2.

Emborg (1988) has described a programme of fatigue tests on 3m prestressed beams having coupled and uncoupled VSL, BBRV and Freyssinet systems with various modifications.

TABLE 5.3

Spliced tendons tested at Braunschweig

Prestressing system	Number of tests	FeP & type of tendon		Fatigue strengths at 2 million cycles N/mm^2
Dyckerhoff & Widmann	6	835/1030	2 x 32mm smooth bars	98
Polensky Zöllner	5	1420/1570	1 x 33 ribbed wires	78
Philipp Holzmann	3	1420/1570	2 x 16 ribbed wires	98
SUSPA/Losinger	3	1570/1770	1 x 12 x 7-wire strands	90

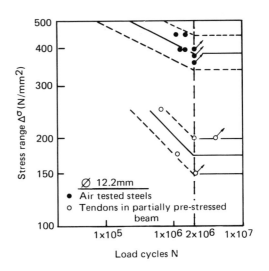

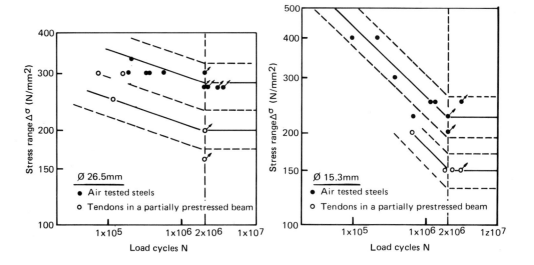

Fig. 5.13
Beams tested at TU Munich
(Müller, 1985, CEB Bulletin No.188)

The standard coupled beams had only 12-15 per cent of the fatigue life of the uncoupled beams. The modifications gave better results but endurances were still far less than those of the uncoupled beams. Fractures were concentrated in the connections and led to the following conclusions.

1   Coupled beams cracked earlier than uncoupled beams because the prestress in the concrete is reduced locally due to creep. Cracking in full-scale coupled structures

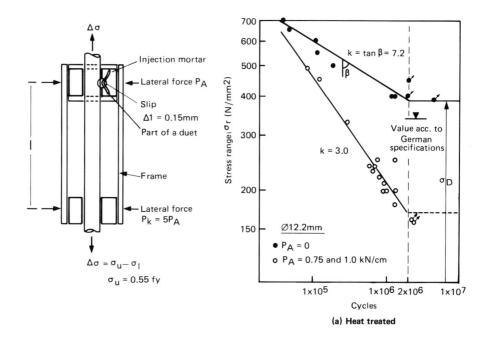

(a) Heat treated

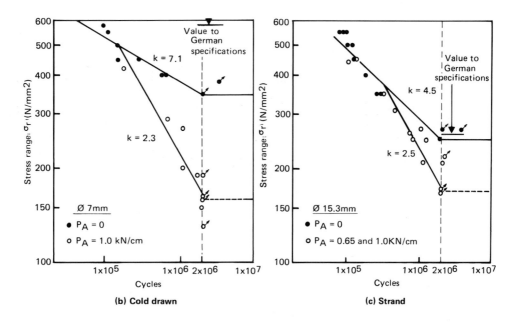

(b) Cold drawn

(c) Strand

Fig. 5.14
Research at RWTH, Aachen
(Cordes and Trost, 1984, CEB Bulletin No.188)

105

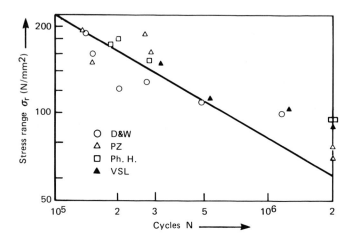

Fig. 5.15
Regression line from
Braunschweig data
(König and Gerhardt, 1986,
CEB Bulletin No.188)

has been attributed to unpredicted bending, temperature stresses and bad workmanship although none of these related to these tests.

2   The low endurance of uncoupled beams compared with that of the same tendons in air is due to fretting against the concrete and also fretting within the coupling unit itself.

3   Local bending may have an important effect by producing stress concentrations and an increase in fretting of tendons.

5.2 Pre-tensioned beams

5.2.1 Railway sleepers

Lambotte and Baus (1963) conducted a series of tests of prestressed railway sleepers. Static failures were in different modes; some in concrete compression, some in shear and some in bond. This confirmed optimal design for static loading but, in the fatigue tests at a lower load level, it was always the tendons that failed in tension.

5.2.2 Rectangular beams - Class 3

Abeles, Brown and Hu (1974) described the failure pattern of under-reinforced prestressed concrete beams with pretensioned and untensioned tendons. Failure was either by brittle fracture of the wires or, if such fatigue failure did not occur, the fatigue loading history did not affect the static strength of the member. The beams were 4.6m long and designed with load factors of 1.5 for dead load and 2.5 for live load. Dead load was 30 per cent and live load was 22 per cent of the static failure load; nominal concrete tensile stress was 4.8 N/mm² under the normal working load of 52 per cent of SFL.

The following conclusions were reached.

1   Generally failure of the beams was not sudden but by the brittle fracture of some tensioned strands one by one.

2   However, under large range loading with σ_{max} due to more than 85 per cent of the static failure load, sudden failure occurred due to crushing of the concrete.

3   Imminent failure was indicated by large deflections and wide cracks.

4   The deflection and cracking depend on bond which is gradually destroyed by fatigue loading.

5   Non-tensioned strands improved the fatigue performance of the beams.

6   Effective prestress gradually decreased until the loss of bond reached a critical point after which it decreased appreciably and crack widths and deflection increased markedly.

7   If bond is good, the fatigue performance of pretensioned strands is as good or better than in air. If bond is poor, the fretting of steel against concrete results in worse fatigue performance than in air.

8   Members designed for 1.5 times dead load plus 2.5 times live load with nominal tensile stress 4.8 N/mm² in the concrete sustained thousands of cycles of loading in the range of 30 to 80 per cent of static failure load and several hundred cycles at 30 to 90 per cent

5.2.3   Inverted T-beams - Class 1

Irwin (1977) has described a test programme at TRRL to study the behaviour of full-scale prestressed concrete bridge beams under static and repetitive loading and the implications of partial prestressing. To be representative of commonly occurring bridges the design used was based upon CCA standard bridge beams, details of which were described by Somerville and Tiller (1970). Three test beams 10.75m long and of T3 standard section as shown in Figure 5.16 were tested in 3-point bending in the rig shown in Figure 5.17. The cube strengths at 28 days were generally in excess of 50 N/mm².

Beam No.1 was subjected firstly to incremental static loading to the point at which a vertical crack had appeared at each transverse hole and then to repeated load cycles with maximum hypothetical tensile stress 70 per cent of the cracking stress and minimum stress at half this level. The maximum stress level was increased ightly to achieve collapse at 3.2 million cycles. Strands failed in the vicinity of the · jor crack as shown in Figure 5.18; seven wires from three strands had fatigue fractu s.

Beam No.2 was not pre-cracked by static loading. Repeated loading was applied with a maximum stress 60 per cent of the cracking stress from Beam No. 1 test. The first crack

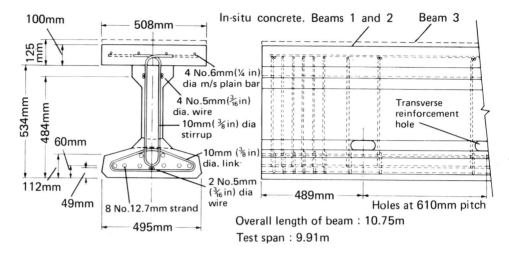

DETAILS OF PRESTRESSED BEAMS AND IN-SITU CONCRETE SLABS

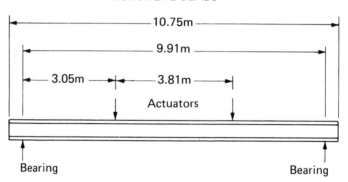

LOADING ARRANGEMENT

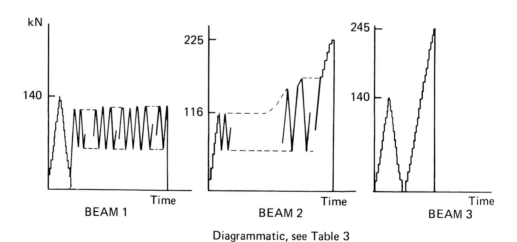

Diagrammatic, see Table 3

LOADING PROGRAMMES

Fig. 5.16
Class 1 inverted T-beams
(Irwin, 1977, LR 802)

108

Fig. 5.17
Beam in the loading rig
(Irwin, 1977, LR 802)

appeared after 300 cycles; after 10,000 cycles there were four and after 4.2 million there were eleven. Collapse was due to two strand failures and the compression failure of the in situ concrete slab shown in Figure 5.19. All except one of the fourteen wires exhibited ductile cup-and-cone failures; the one centre wire showed a flat complex fracture surface typical of fatigue.

Beam No.3 was provided with a thicker in situ flange than Beams Nos. 1 and 2. Static test loading was applied in two stages; the first to establish the crack pattern and the second was continued to collapse. In addition to the flexure cracks in the constant moment section this beam developed flexure-shear cracks in the shear spans (also present in Beam No.2) and web shear cracks, one of which near a support propagated to the top of the precast beam as shown in Figure 5.20(a). Failure of wires in the upper web and pull-out of stirrups resulted in the separation of the in situ slab from the beam. The separation progressed inwards pand resulted in the web compression failure shown in Figure 5.20(b).

Distributions of longitudinal strain are plotted in Figure 5.21 and the load, moment and curvature in Figure 5.22.

109

Fig. 5.18
Beam 1 prior to collapse
(Irwin, 1977, LR 802)

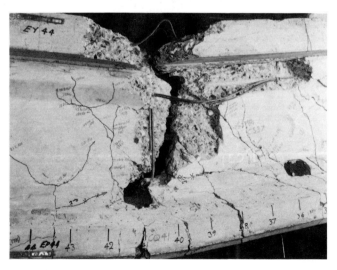

Fig. 5.19
Beam 2 after collapse
(Irwin, 1977, LR 802)

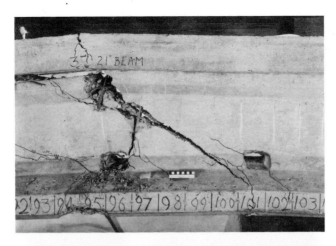

Fig. 5.20
Beam 3 after collapse
(Irwin, 1977, LR 802)

The following conclusions were drawn.

1   When there was no tensile stress at the soffit the prestressed beams behaved elastically and fatigue is unlikely under this limitation.

2   When there is tensile stress at the soffit fatigue failure could be brought about by a sufficient number of repetitions.

3   Fatigue failure of Beam No.1 after 3.2 million cycles was at a load about 37 per cent above the Class 1 serviceability limit and about equal to the Class 2 limit. The breakdown of bond was an important factor.

4   The collapse load of Beam No.2 was about twice the calculated ultimate load.

5   The collapse load of Beam No.3 was about twice the calculated ultimate load in bending and more than twice that in shear.

111

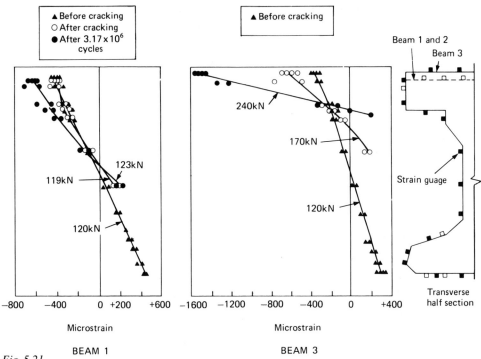

Fig. 5.21
Longitudinal strain
(Irwin, 1977, LR 802)

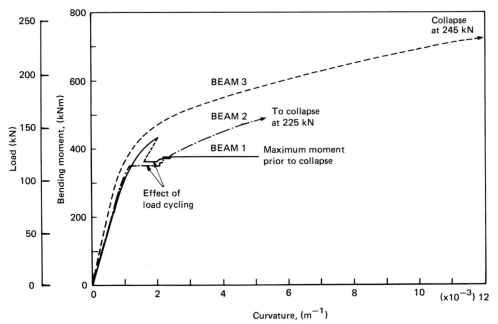

Fig. 5.22
Load, moment and curvature
(Irwin, 1977, LR 802)

112

6   Similar beams subjected to more than 3 million repetitions of loading to Class 2 limitations may suffer fatigue failure.

5.2.4 Lightweight concrete beams - Class 1

Howells and Raithby (1977) reported a similar test programme on lightweight aggregate concrete beams from the long-line production run for Redesdale Bridge. This experimental bridge was designed under the author's supervision, for the Forestry Commission who undertook the site construction. Casting of the bridge deck is shown in Figure 5.23. The precasting and site works were monitored by TRRL.

Fig. 5.23
Construction of Redesdale Bridge
(Howells and Raithby, 1977, LR 804)

The beams were 17.37m long having the standard T7 cross-section with a deep top flange shown in Figure 5.24. Both the precast beams and the in situ slab were made with Lytag aggregate concrete with density and 28 day cube strength as given in Table 5.4.

The test rig is shown in Figures 5.25 and 5.26.

One beam was loaded statically to establish the cracking load and the ultimate load. Failure was in compression after buckling of the deck slab.

The next beam was subjected to 2 million cycles at load levels increasing up to 70 per cent

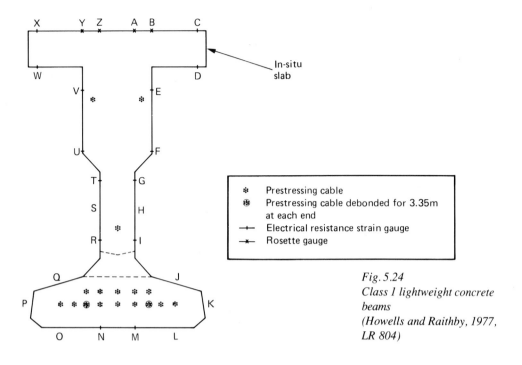

X Y Z A B C

In-situ
slab

W V E D

U F

T G

S H

R I

	Prestressing cable
⊕	Prestressing cable debonded for 3.35m at each end
⊢	Electrical resistance strain gauge
✳	Rosette gauge

Q J

P K

O N M L

Fig. 5.24
Class 1 lightweight concrete
beams
(Howells and Raithby, 1977,
LR 804)

TABLE 5.4

Lightweight aggregate concrete

	Density (kg/m³)	*Cube strength (N/mm²)*
Precast beams	1860	54
In situ concrete	1780	41

of ultimate with relatively few cycles at the higher stress levels. Finally it was loaded to failure by static incremental loading.

A third beam was subjected to cyclic loading from 12 to 60 per cent of ultimate to failure. Some wires in the lower strands failed in fatigue after 289,000 cycles compared with about 250,000 predicted from the literature. The appearance of the strand failure can be seen in Figure 5.27.

The following conclusions were drawn.

1   Collapse under static loading resulted from buckling of the deck slab followed by compression failure of the flange.

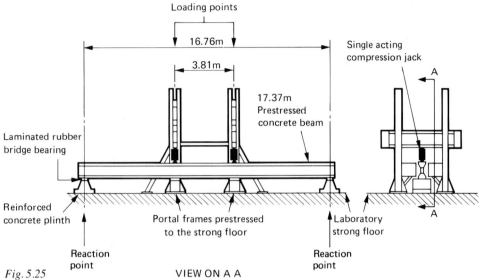

Loading points

16.76m

3.81m

17.37m
Prestressed
concrete beam

Single acting
compression jack

Laminated rubber
bridge bearing

Reinforced
concrete plinth

Portal frames prestressed
to the strong floor

Laboratory
strong floor

Reaction
point

Reaction
point

VIEW ON A A

Fig. 5.25
Test rig used for lightweight concrete beams
(Howells and Raithby, 1977, LR 804)

Fig. 5.26
Bridge beam set up for loading
test
(Howells and Raithby, 1977,
LR 804)

115

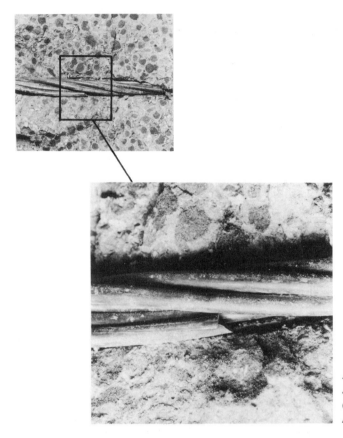

*Fig. 5.27
Detail of strand failure
(Howells and Raithby, 1977,
LR 804)*

2   Tensile cracks appeared consistently at about 42 per cent of the static collapse load when the concrete reached about 230 microstrain.

3   The maximum crack width was 0.2 mm at 60 per cent ultimate load.

4   Under fatigue loading the onset of cracking agreed well with predictions made on the basis of curves for normal concrete.

5   The failure characteristics of the lightweight concrete under both static and repetitive loading were more brittle than normal concrete with cracks passing through the aggregate. See also 2.3.1.

6   Cyclic loading from 12 to 60 per cent of ultimate resulted in fatigue failure of several prestressing wires at 289,000 cycles after extensive transverse and longitudinal cracking of the surrounding concrete.

7   Fatigue failure of the tendons agreed closely with the life predicted from published data and was similar in nature to that in conventional prestressed beams of similar design.

5.3 Vertical shear in composite beams

Price and Edwards (1971) tested shear cracking of prestressed beams under repeated loading at Imperial College. The I-section beams were 152 mm wide by 356 mm deep with 38 mm reinforced webs. One beam was tested with the maximum load level at 56 per cent and the minimum at 25 per cent of the static ultimate shear strength. This produced maximum principal tensile stresses in the web of 1.93 N/mm^2 and 0.48 N/mm^2. Compared with the tensile strength of 2.59 N/mm^2 the maximum and minimum tensile stress levels were 75 and 19 per cent respectively and that loading caused inclined cracking in the web after 1,696,000 cycles. Another beam cycled at 74 and 19 per cent of the tensile strength of the web concrete sustained 3,088,000 repetitions without the incidence of inclined cracking. It was concluded that the fatigue strength of concrete in the webs of prestressed beams at 3 million cycles is about 75 per cent of the static tensile strength.

Fatigue tests of reinforced concrete beams by Ruhnau (1974) showed that the tensile stress in the stirrups increased under repeated loading which left a residual stress 15 to 30 per cent of yield.

Ueda and Okamura (1981) carried out shear tests on reinforced concrete T-beams under multi-level cyclic loading. Strain gauge measurements on the stirrups led to the following conclusions.

1   The maximum strain in the stirrups increased with the number of cycles and with increasing range of loading under a constant maximum. This was due to the decreased amount of shear carried by the concrete.

2   The strain range under constant load range increased with the number of cycles and there was a significant residual strain.

Bennett, Cusens and Tay (1985) tested four composite beams 8 m long comprising precast prestressed concrete MoT/CCA bridge beams, section M5, with in situ concrete deck slab as shown in Figure 5.28.

The precast beams were prestressed with 25-15.2 mm strands to give concrete stresses at transfer of 17 N/mm^2 compression at the soffit and 1 N/mm^2 at the top of the pre-cast unit. Shear reinforcement was 8 mm Torbar at 125 mm centres as shown in Figure 5.29. To simulate tack welded longitudinal lacing bars in three of the beams short lengths of 8mm Torbar were welded in the positions indicated.

Each beam was first loaded statically in 3-point bending on a span of 7.5 m to the upper level of the repetitive loading to be applied. Deflection and strain measurements were taken at load increments and this procedure was repeated during interruptions of the repeated loading which was at frequencies between 0.28 and 0.58 Hz.

The following conclusions were reached.

1   Inclined cracking of the web occurred after 1 million cycles of a principal tensile

117

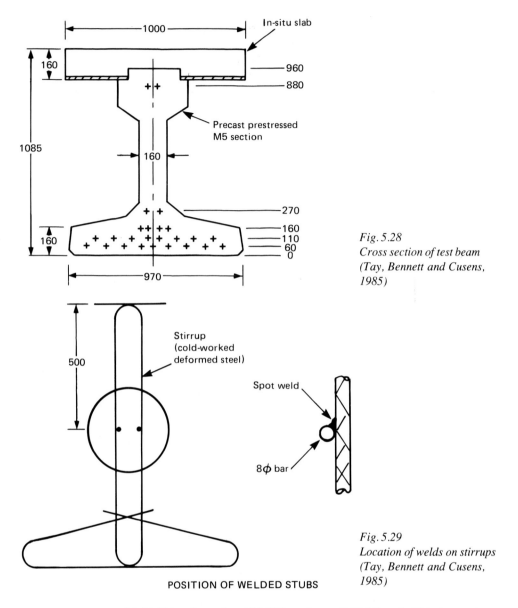

Fig. 5.28
Cross section of test beam
(Tay, Bennett and Cusens, 1985)

POSITION OF WELDED STUBS

Fig. 5.29
Location of welds on stirrups
(Tay, Bennett and Cusens, 1985)

stress range of 2.11 N/mm² or after 100,000 cycles at 2.73 N/mm². This is consistent with the tensile fatigue behaviour of plain concrete.

2   The inclination of cracks was similar to that caused by static loading but the maximum crack widths were rather greater.

3   The width of cracks increased considerably under repeated loading, sometimes to almost double before fatigue failure of the stirrups.

4   In the unlikely event of frequent repetition of the full service load, fatigue cracking could occur in beams designed to current shear rules.

5   Before cracking the stress in the stirrups was negligible. After the onset of inclined cracking in the webs, the stress in the stirrups increased with the number of load repetitions.

6   The increase of cyclic stress in stirrups follows the characteristic model:

$$\sigma_{sv} = \sigma_{sv\ min} + (V - V_{sv\ min\ o})\ s_v\ \tan\theta / A_{sv} d$$

   s_v is stirrup spacing (mm)

   A is stirrup cross-sectional area (mm^2)

   d is the effective depth of section (mm)

   σ_v is the stress in the stirrups (N/mm^2)

   θ is the angle of inclination of cracks to the horizontal

   V is the ultimate shear force (N)

   V_{sv} is the shear force carried by the stirrups (N)

7   The maximum and residual stress in the stirrups increased with repeated loading, the maximum stress sometimes approaching yield.

8   Failure of stirrups was due to fatigue, accelerated by the increased stress level during loading, and was always where the stirrup crossed a web crack.

9   In one test no fatigue failure of stirrups had occurred in 2.7 million cycles after cracking, the average cyclic stress near the cracks was initially from 150 N/mm^2 to 250 N/mm^2 and increased by about 30 N/mm^2.

10   The extent to which shear fatigue strength was reduced by tack welding was not determined. Fatigue failure was not restricted to weld positions but was mainly dependent on the position of cracks. Therefore the detrimental effect was less than that found from tests in air. Nevertheless tack welding to stirrups in the webs of beams subject to fatigue is considered to be inadvisable. Examples of fractures are shown in Figures 5.30, 5.31 and 5.32.

Fig. 5.30
Fracture of stirrup at tack weld
(Tay, Bennett and Cusens, 1985)

120

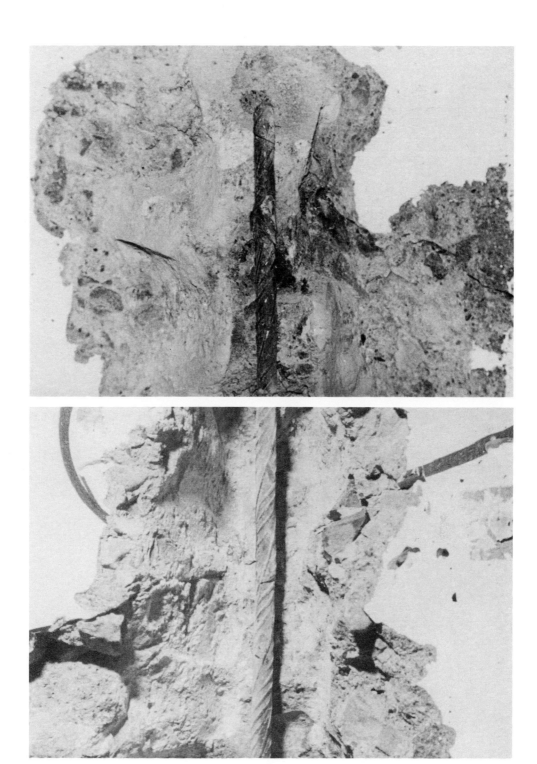

Figure 5.31
Fracture of stirrup remote from tack weld
(Tay, Bennett and Cusens, 1985)

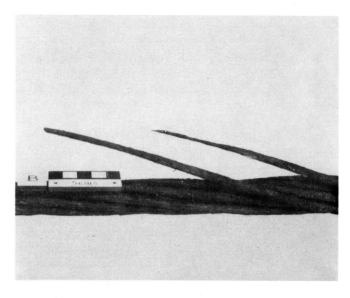

Fig. 5.32
Corroded 19-wire strand
removed from bridge after 21
years
(Tilly, Durability of concrete
bridges. IHT Journal, Feb.
1988)

5.4 Summary

Fatigue is not a problem in prestressed concrete in which there is no cracking, that is Class 1 or 2 with no deterioration.

The characteristic regression line for fatigue of prestressing strand is given in Figure 5.3. Different prestressing steels have fatigue strengths at 2 million cycles as given in Figure 5.4.

Fretting reduces fatigue performance and can occur between:

- the wires of a strand

- tendon and voided duct

- wires and anchorages

Corrosion pitting reduces fatigue performance; observed effects on bar and wire and strand are plotted in Figures 5.7, 5.9 and 5.9.

The fatigue strength of tendons in concrete can be 40 to 70 per cent lower than in air.

Couplers have lower fatigue strength than bare tendons; sometimes as little as 12 per cent.

Fatigue strengths of different types of prestressing steel in Table 5.5 are based on the research summarised in Table 4.8 of CEB Bulletin No.188. Values in brackets relate to fretting for endurances greater than 1 million. See 6.3.5. Values relate to uncorroded prestressing steel. If pitting corrosion is present, a reduction factor must be applied. Tilly

TABLE 5.5

Characteristic fatigue strength of prestressing steel

Prestressing steel Type and condition		σ_{rk} (N/mm²) for N million cycles			Stress exponent m
		N = 1	N = 2	N = 10	
Hot rolled	smooth	280 (110)	260	220 (70)	7 (5)
	threaded	200 (80)	190	170 (70)	13 (13)
Heat treated	smooth	300 (120)	280	230 (75)	7 (5)
	ribbed	250 (100)	230	195 (63)	7 (5)
Cold drawn	smooth	200 (80)	185	155 (50)	7 (5)
	profiled	200 (80)	185	155 (50)	7 (5)
	strand	200 (80)	180	140 (50)	4 (5)

(1988) proposed a factor of 1.35 from tests on strands which had lost 5 to 15 per cent of cross section.

More severely corroded strands, in which more than one wire had failed, were recovered from the same source but were not tested. It is reasonable to apply a factor of 1.7 in such cases as for reinforcing bars.

Pretensioned beams generally have a gradual failure mode under fatigue loading as tendons fracture one by one. Failure is preceded by increasing deflection and crack widths. However, under large range cycles with the maximum greater than 85 per cent of the static ultimate strength, sudden failure can occur due to crushing of the concrete. Fatigue behaviour depends very much on bond.

The fatigue strength at 3 million cycles of a composite prestressed beam designed for static loading is about 37 per cent above the Class 1 serviceability limit or equal to the Class 2 serviceability limit. This strength is about 70 per cent of the cracking strength.

Lightweight aggregate concrete beams behave similarly to normal concrete but cracking tends to pass through aggregate instead of around the particles and failure tends to be more brittle.

5.5 References

ABELES, P W, BROWN, E I and HU, C H (1974) Fatigue resistance of under-reinforced prestressed beams subjected to different stress ranges; Miner's Hypothesis. ACI Publication SP-41-11 12, pp237-278 and 279-300.

ANDREWS, A E and TURNER, F H (1985) Post-tensioning systems for concrete in the UK 1940-1985. CIRIA Report No.106.

BAUS, R and BRENNEISEN, A (1968) The fatigue strength of prestressing steel. FIP Symposium, Madrid.

BEALES, C and IVES D I (1990). Behaviour of permanent formwork. TRRL Report RR254.

BENNETT, E W, CUSENS A R and TAY C J. Vertical shear strength of composite prestressed concrete bridge beams: M beam with added deck slab. TRRL Contractor Report CR174.

CANTELI, A, ESSLINGER, V and THÜRLIMANN, B (1984) Ermüdungsfesigkeit von Bewehrungs- und Spannstählen. Institut für Baustatik und Konstruktion, ETH, Zürich.

CORDES, H and TROST, H (1984) Investigation on the fatigue strength of prestressing tendons under the special conditions of partial prestressing. Research Workshop (A.R.W.) on partial prestressing. Paris.

CULLIMORE, M S G (1972) The fatigue strength of high tensile steel wire cable subjected to stress fluctuations of small amplitude. IABSE Publications pp49-56

EDWARDS, A D and PICARD, A (1972) Fatigue characteristics of prestressing strand. Proceedings. Institution of Civil Engineers. 53 Part 2. pp325-336.

EMBORG, M (1988) Fatigue strength of cable couplers in prestressed concrete beams. Nordisk betong 2-3.

ENDO, K, GOTO, H and NAKAMURA, T (1969) Effects of cycle frequency on fretting fatigue life of carbon steel. Bulletin of ISME, Bd. 12 No. 54, pp1300-1308.

ERDMANN, J, KORDINA, K and NEISECKE, I (1982) Auswertung von Berichten uber Abbrucharbeiten von Spannbeton-Bauwerken im Hinblick auf das Langzeitverhalten von Spannstählen. Forschungsbericht T 1172, IRB Verlag-Stuttgart.

FUNK, W (1969) Ein Prüfverfahren zur Untersuchung des Einflusses der Reibkorrosion auf die Dauerhaltbarkeit, Materialprüfung 11, Nr 7.

HOWELLS, H and RAITHBY, K D (1977) Static and repeated loading tests on light-weight prestressed concrete bridge beams. TRRL Laboratory Report 804.

IRWIN, C A K (1977) Static and repetitive loading tests on full-scale prestressed concrete bridge beams. TRRL Report LR802.

KORDINA, K and GÜNTHER, J (1982) Dauerschwellversuche an Koppelankern unter praxisähnlichen Bedingungen, Bauingenieur 57/1982, pp103-108.

LAMBOTTE, H and BAUS (1963) Experimental study of the effect of fatigue on the behaviour of reinforced concrete beams. Revue C. Nos. 3 4.

LONGBOTTOM, K W and MALLETT, G P (1973) Prestressing steels. Journal of the Institution of Structural Engineers, vol 51, No. 12, pp445-471.

MANTON,B H and WILSON, C B (1971) MoT/CCA standard bridge beams. Prestressed inverted T-beams for spans from 15 to 29 m. Cement and Concrete Association.

MÜLLER, H H (1985) Prüfverfahren fur die Dauerfestigkeit von Spannstählen, Bericht Nr.1111, Lehrstuhl für Massivbau, TU Munchen.

NEUBERT, B and NÜRNBERGER, U (1983) Beurteilung des dynamischen Tragverhaltens von Spannstählen in Abhängigkeit von Rostgrad, Bericht der FMPA Baden-Wurttemberg Nr.II.6-13675 im Rahmen des BMFT Forschungsvorhabens Spatsschaden an Spannbetonbauteilen Prophylaxe, Früherkennung, Behebung.

NÜRNBERGER, U (1981) Dauerschwingverhalten von Spannstählen. Bauingenieur 56 pp311-319.

PAULSON, C, FRANK, K H and BREEN, J E (1983) A fatigue study of prestressing strand. Center for Transportation Research. University of Texas at Austin Research Report 300-1.

PRICE, K M and EDWARDS, A D (1971) Fatigue strength in shear of prestressed concrete I-beams. ACI Journal, 68-31, pp282-292.

RIGON, C and THÜRLIMANN, B Fatigue tests on post-tensioned concrete beams. Versuchsbericht Nr. 8101-1 Institut fur Baustatik und Konstruktion, ETH Zürich

RUHNAU, J (1974) Influence of repeated loading on the stirrup stress of reinforced concrete beams. Shear in Reinforced Concrete, Vol.1, ACI Publication SP-42, pp 169-181.

SOMERVILLE, G and TILLER, R M (1970) Standard bridge beams for spans from 7 m to 36 m. Cement and Concrete Association Publication 46.005. London.

TIDE, R H R and VAN HORN, D A (1966) A statistical study of the static and fatigue properties of high strength prestressing strand. Report 309.2 Fritz Engineering Laboratory. Lehigh University.

TILLY, G P (1988) Durability of concrete bridges. Journal of the Institution of Highways and Transportation, February.

TILLY, G P (1988) Performance of bridge cables. Session 4, 1st Oleg Kerensky Memorial Conference. London.

UEDA, T and OKAMURA, H (1981) Behaviour of stirrups under fatigue loading. Reprint from Transactions of the Japan Concrete Institute, Vol. 3.

WOODWARD, R J (1981) Conditions within ducts in post-tensioned prestressed concrete bridges. TRRL Report LR980.

6. Design and assessment rules

6.1 Introduction

The Limit State of Fatigue is considered under the following headings:

1   Loading

2   Material properties

3   Structural analysis

4   Assessment principles

5   Application

6   Inspection

Fatigue damage, consisting of the propagation of cracks in a structural member, is caused by repeated application of the same or varied loading cycles. Fatigue failure is considered to be an Ultimate Limit State which is rendered acceptably improbable if the number and/or stress range of cycles of service loading would not cause excessive cumulative damage at critical features of the structure.

6.2 Loading

Low-cycle fatigue would be brought about by a relatively small number of cycles of loading at levels approaching the static failure load for the member. This is virtually precluded by proper design for static loads but could become the mode of failure in association with massive deterioration or earthquake loading. Low-cycle fatigue is usually considered to be up to 10,000 cycles.

High-cycle fatigue performance may be assessed on the basis of the known or estimated numbers of loading cycles applied to a structural member in the course of its service life.

The simplest case would be a single repeated loading action such as that due to machinery with no other loading of sufficient magnitude to have an effect on fatigue life.

More commonly, service loading is represented by a spectrum of certain numbers of cycles of various specified intensities such as numbers of vehicles of certain weights or waves of various heights. For example loading spectra for highway bridges and railway bridges are given in BS 5400:Part 10:1980. Fatigue analysis of marine structures has been well described by Price, Hambly and Tricklebank (1989).

The most sophisticated treatment involves monitoring random loading actions such as wind gusting or wave action. Random data can be expressed as the sum of simple harmonic functions which can then be processed by either of two methods: deterministic or spectral. In the first method the structural response wave by wave is assumed to be linear and unaffected by the stress history of the element. In the spectral method the structural response is derived from data using spectral density functions and transfer functions.

6.3 Material properties

6.3.1   Specifications

Structural grade concrete is specified by various authorities, in various British Standards, such as BS 5400:Part 7 for bridges, and also by CEN, the European Committee for Standardisation, for cement testing and concrete performance criteria.

Carbon steel bar reinforcement is specified in BS 4449:1988 and in EU 80; cold reduced wire reinforcement in BS 4482:1985 and steel fabric reinforcement in BS 4483:1985.

Cold worked steel bar reinforcement was specified in BS 4461. Although the standard was withdrawn in 1988 this type of steel is in existing structures and has to be considered for assessment purposes.

High tensile prestressing wire and strand are specified in BS 5896:1980 and hot rolled bar for prestressing in BS 4486:1988.

6.3.2   The CEB-FIP Model Code (1990)

The CEB-FIP Model Code (1990) as presented in Bulletin No 190 gives rules for assessing the Ultimate Limit State of Fatigue where there will be more than 10,000 repetitions and does not cover low-cycle fatigue. The criteria do not always coincide with those proposed from the original research but were developed in the light of CEB Bulletin No.188. Characteristic fatigue strength functions have been given and maximum cycle stresses must be multiplied by the appropriate partial safety factors before using them to calculate fatigue life. This does not apply to γ_M for material variability which is already included in the functions. The Model Code parameters are adopted here in the main but there are two significant differences in presentation.

127

The Model Code gives three methods, increasing in refinement with the Palmgren-Miner summation of spectrum loading as the most sophisticated. Here it is convenient first to consider fatigue strengths with rigorous assessment and then to offer conservative rules that satisfy the criteria.

The Model Code defines fatigue strengths at 10 million cycles after which the stress exponent, m, is increased to m + 2. The research suggests flattening of the S-N curve for prestressing steels at 1 million cycles.

6.3.3 Fatigue strength of concrete

Concrete in compression:

$$\log N = 10 \ (\ 1 - (\sigma_{max}/f_{cm}))/(\ 1 - R\ )^{1/2}$$

Concrete in compression-tension; $\sigma\tau_{max} < 0.2 \ \sigma_{max}$ and compression failure:

$$\log N = 9 \ (1 - (\sigma_{max}/f_{cm}))$$

Concrete in tension:

$$\log N = 10 \ (\ 1 - (\sigma_{tmax}/f_{ctm}))$$

6.3.4 Fatigue strength of steel reinforcement

Characteristic fatigue strength functions for steel reinforcement are of the form:

$$(\sigma_r)^m \ N = k \text{ or } \log N = C - m \log r \text{ as given in Figure 6.1 and Table 6.1.}$$

The values given are for uncorroded steel. If steel has pitting corrosion, a reduction factor of 1.35 should be applied for up to 25 per cent loss of section or 1.7 for more than 25 per cent loss of section.

Lapped joints with unbent bars have the fatigue strength of continuous bar; if bars are cranked a reduction factor of 2.0 should be applied.

6.3.5 Fatigue strength of prestressing steel:

Parameters for the different types of prestressing steel are given in Figure 6.2 and Table 6.2 which is a simplification of Table 5.5. Values in brackets relate to fretting for endurances greater than 1 million cycles. At lesser endurances the normal stress exponent for the particular material should be used.

S-N lines corresponding to Table 6.2 are plotted on Figure 6.2. together with the Model Code S-N lines. The values given are for uncorroded steel. If steel has pitting corrosion,

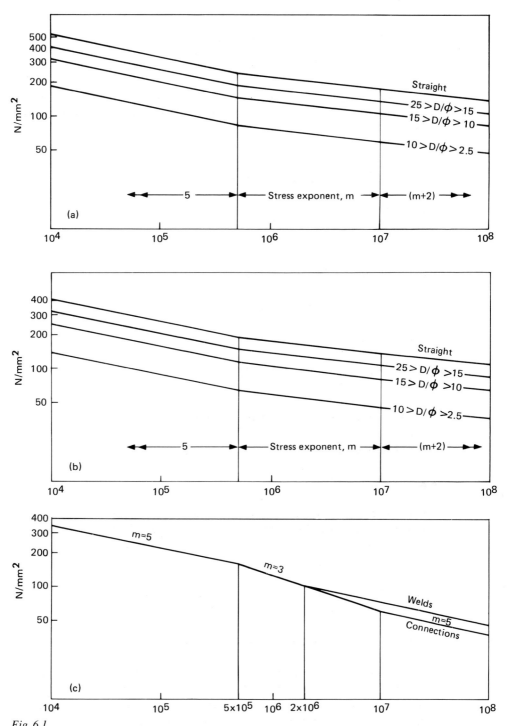

Fig. 6.1
(a) Characteristic fatigue strength of steel reinforcement with diameters up to 16mm
(b) Characteristic fatigue strength of steel reinforcement with diameters greater than 16mm
(c) Characteristic fatigue strength of mechanical connections and welds in steel reinforcement

TABLE 6.1

Characteristic fatigue strength of steel reinforcement

Reinforcing steel size and condition	σ_{rk} (N/mm^2) at 10 million cycles	Stress exponent m
Ø < 16 mm straight bars	175	9*
bent 25 > D/Ø ≥ 15	135	9*
15 > D/Ø ≥ 10	105	9*
10 > D/Ø ≥ 2.5	60	9*
Ø > 16 mm straight bars	135	9*
bent 25 > D/Ø ≥ 15	105	9*
15 > D/Ø ≥ 10	80	9*
10 > D/Ø ≥ 2.5	45	9*
Mechanical connections	60 at 2 million cycles	3*
Butt welds or tack welds	100	3**

* except for N < 500,000 use m = 5 and for N > 10 million use (m + 2)
** except for N < 500,000 use m = 5 and for N > 2 million use (m + 2)

TABLE 6.2

Characteristic fatigue strength of prestressing steel

Prestressing steel Type and condition	σ_{rk} (N/mm^2) for N million cycles			Stress exponent m
	N = 1	N = 2	N = 10	
Smooth bar	280 (110)	260	220 (70)	7 (5)
Ribbed bar	250 (100)	230	195 (63)	7 (5)
Threaded bar	200 (80)	190	170 (70)	13 (13)
Cold drawn wire	200 (80)	185	155 (50)	7 (5)
Strand	200 (80)	180	140 (50)	4 (5)
All types in voided ducts	(80)	-	- (50)	- (5)

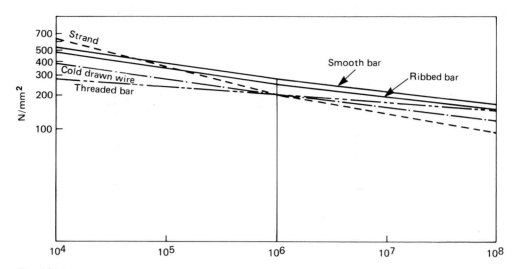

Fig.6.2(a)
Characteristic fatigue strength of prestressing steels

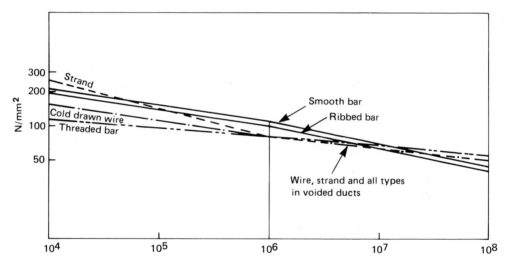

Fig.6.2(b)
Characteristic fatigue strength of prestressing steels subject to fretting

a reduction factor of 1.35 should be applied for up to 25 per cent loss of section or 1.7 for more than 25 per cent loss of section.

6.4 Structural analysis

Some aspects of calculating stresses in reinforced and prestressed concrete members under fatigue loading (from CEB Bulletin No.188) will be found in Appendix 5.

6.5 Assessment principles

6.5.1 Rigorous assessment

A full assessment of the fatigue performance of a structure requires the following steps:

1 State the service life required

2 Determine the number and intensity of all load cycles in that life

3 Identify the most fatigue sensitive features of the structure

4 For each feature calculate:

  the stress range due to each load cycle

  n, the number of these cycles in the life

  N, the endurance for this stress range from S-N data

  the Palmgren/Miner summation Σ n/N $=\omega$

 If unacceptable, amend design

 If acceptable, continue to next feature

5 Guidance on the value of the ω criterion and sample calculations will be found in Appendix 4.

6 Counting methods for variable amplitude loading are described in Appendix 3.

The process is shown in the form of a flow chart in Figure 6.3.

6.5.2 Limitations deemed to satisfy the fatigue requirements

The Model Code defines the following criteria to avoid the need for fatigue calculations. They are necessarily more conservative than a full fatigue assessment.

Concrete. The maximum calculated factored stress range does not exceed the appropriate value taken from the following.

Compression	0.25 times the static compressive strength.
Compression-tension	0.18 times the static compressive strength.
Tension	0.25 times the static tensile strength.

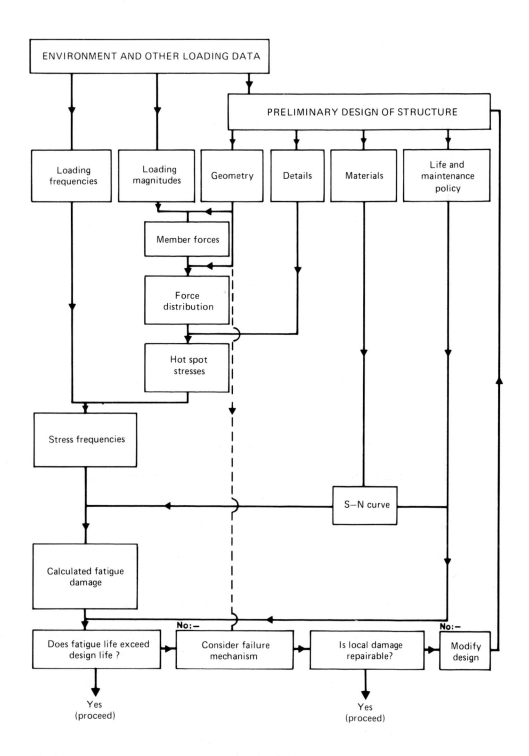

Fig. 6.3
Flow diagram of fatigue analysis procedure
(Price, Tricklebank and Hambly, 1982)

133

Steel. The number of cycles, n, does not exceed 10 million and the maximum calculated factored stress range does not exceed the appropriate fatigue strength at 10 million cycles taken from the following values.

Maximum stress range (N/mm²)

Reinforcing steel:

Land based structures	100
Marine structures	35

Prestressing steel:

Fully bonded	60
In ungrouted ducts	45

6.5.3   Constant amplitude loading

If the loading is of constant amplitude the fatigue requirements will be met if the maximum calculated stress range does not exceed the appropriate fatigue strength from 6.3.

6.6   Application to bridges

6.6.1   Loading spectra

BS 5400:Part 10:1980 gives load spectra for both highway bridges and railway bridges derived from the analysis of traffic data on typical roads and rail routes. For highways, it defines the total numbers of vehicles over 30 kN total weight to be assumed annually in each lane of roads of various categories and a table of 25 commercial vehicles with their axle weights and spacings so that a realistic proportion of each type is taken. This commercial traffic was taken as 20 per cent of the total traffic on all-purpose roads and 25 per cent on motorways. The design life is taken to be 120 years.

Seifert (1989) described a procedure using up-to-date European traffic data and computer simulation. Using data from the average daily lorry flows listed in Table 6.3, he constructed the profiles of axle loads and gross truck weights shown in Figure 6.4 (a) and (b). The effect of load on a particular structural detail can be presented as a standard spectrum as illustrated in Figure 6.5. The attraction of this technique is that the program, once set up, can be updated to take account of changes in vehicle weights, the proportions of various vehicles or total traffic flow.

134

TABLE 6.3

Daily lorry flows

Brohltal	D	6600	1984
Auxerre	F	2400	1986
Périphérique	F	5107	1983
Forth	GB	1350	1978
Doxey	GB	8482*	1985

* including small vans; all others exceed 35 kN gross

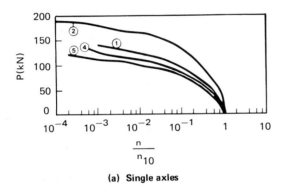

(a) Single axles

(b) Trucks

Fig. 6.4
Axle loads and gross truck weights
(Seifert, 1989)

6.6.2 Simplified procedures

BS 5400:Part 10:1980 offers an alternative to rigorous assessment where the standard loading spectrum applies.

Instead of having 25 different axle configurations to traverse the influence line, a single standard fatigue vehicle of 320 kN total weight on 4 axles is applied and the resulting stress range is then compared with the limiting stress range taken from a graph for the

135

Standard Spectrum of Effects

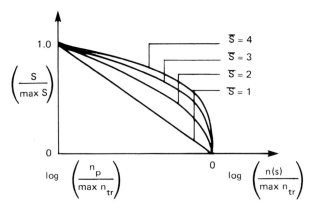

Corresponding Probability Density Function
(Continuous representation of the histogram)

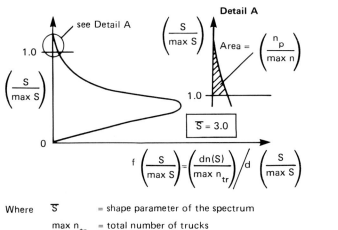

Where $\overline{S}$ = shape parameter of the spectrum

max n_{tr} = total number of trucks

max S = maximum effect

n_p = number of cycles with at least
the amplitude max S

Fig. 6.5
Spectrum of effects and
density functions
(Seifert, 1989)

relevant structural detail, category of road and value of L. L is the base length of the portion of the point load influence line which contains the greatest ordinate. Limiting stress range graphs for unwelded reinforcing bars, R1 and R2 are shown in Figure 6.6.

A rather more precise alternative method using the standard fatigue vehicle to estimate the fatigue damage is given in BS 5400:Part 10:1980 for various steel bridge details using a damage chart which includes welded reinforcing bars but not unwelded bars.

Hambly carried out a series of fatigue analyses for TRRL with abitrary but realistic influence line loop lengths,L, in the range 1 to 200 m and proposed conservative limits for stress range to avoid the need for a detailed assessment. The values of stress range

136

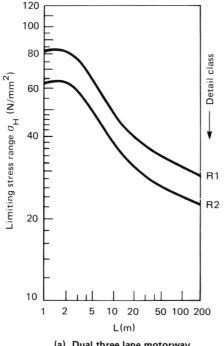

(a) Dual three lane motorway

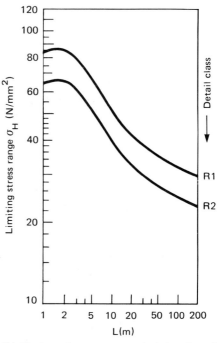

(b) Dual two lane motorway, dual three lane all purpose, dual two lane all purpose

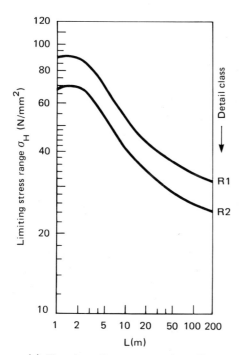

(c) Three lane all purpose, two lane all purpose (10m), two lane slip road

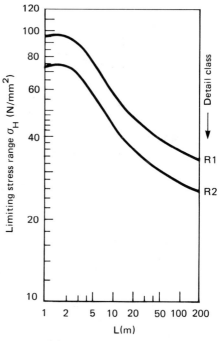

(d) Two lane all purpose (7.3m); single lane slip road

Fig. 6.6
Limiting stress range for unwelded reinforcing bars
(Hambly, 1989)

are 155 N/mm² for reinforcing bars up to 16 mm, 120 N/mm² for larger bars and 50 N/mm² for severely corroded bars.

Hambly (1989) studied the effects of tack welding and proposed 140 N/mm² as a conservative highest calculated stress range to avoid a full fatigue assessment as a Class D detail.

6.6.3   Assessing present fatigue damage

The Case Studies listed in Chapter 1 show that fatigue was only one of the contributing causes of failure in those concrete structures. Since the 1950s, it has been the practice in the United Kingdom and elsewhere to use salt on roads for de-icing; this has caused widespread damage to concrete highway structures. If reinforcing steel or prestressing steel suffer pitting corrosion, the loss of section increases stress levels and thence the risk of static or fatigue failure.

From inspection, sampling and measurements, the present cross sectional area of the steel can be estimated; then the present stresses and future fatigue life can be calculated. If this leads to the decision to replace the structure, its fatigue history is only of academic interest. However, if it is necessary to keep the damaged steel in service, its present fatigue damage has to be estimated.

In the absence of evidence otherwise, it will be on the safe side to assume that concrete cover provides effective protection for 15 years and that loss of section from pitting corrosion occurs thereafter at a uniform rate per year.

The assessment also requires assumptions about traffic loading in past years. The fatigue spectrum of BS 5400:Part 10:1980 was derived from weighbridge data taken between 1971 and 1974. Almost all fatigue damage to highway bridges is caused by heavy lorries, the mileage of which increased quite dramatically between 1955 and 1979 as described by Armitage (1980). It can be assumed that no fatigue damage was caused before 1955 and that the numbers and configurations of vehicles given in the BS 5400:Part10:1980 spectrum are applicable from 1975 onwards, having increased uniformly to those values from zero in 1955.

Fatigue damage can then be assessed for each decade of the structure after age 15, using values of cross section and loading spectrum interpolated to the end of that decade.

6.7   Design, inspection and hot spots

Whether he is designing a structure or assessing a structure in service, the engineer must judge whether or not it is susceptible to fatigue and, if it is, which are its vulnerable details - or hot spots. Although concrete is capable of redistributing stress concentrations, reliance should not be placed on this where loading is repetitive. Resonant loading cycles are particularly damaging. Stresses may be modified by creep, loss of bond or cracking.

Hot spots are stress concentrations such as:

1   changes of section

2   member connections

3   bearings and joints

4   holes and notches

5   anchorages and couplers

6   butt and tack welds.

Normally, in tensile zones, cracks should be fine, closely spaced and hardly perceptible by virtue of well designed reinforcement.

It is necessary to distinguish two types of cracking.

1   in a tensile zone associated with a compression zone, as in a beam

2   in a fully tensile zone, as in a tie.

In the first case, fatigue assessment as uniaxial compression will be conservative because there is a reserve of strength due to the stress gradient.

Excessive cracking may be due to:

1   under-design

2   over-loading

3   damaged steel

4   damaged concrete

5   loss of prestress

6   shrinkage

Cracks may have been caused by an exceptional loading, seldom, if ever, to be repeated, or they may be opening and closing under service conditions.

Plain concrete may fatigue in compression, tension, tension-compression or compression-tension. See 2.2 and 2.3.1.

Increasing moisture content reduces fatigue strength.

Static compression preloading and rest periods both improve performance.

The bending fatigue performance of an under-reinforced member is governed by the steel. More heavily reinforced members may have failure modes in bending or shear or bond.

The stress in stirrups is increased where they are crossed by inclined shear cracks; stress may also be critical at bends or welds.

Effective bond is very important. If bond is adequate, the failure mode is by principal tension in the surrounding concrete, taking more cycles than the endurance at that constant maximum cycling stress. Inadequate bond leads to "zipper" type failure along the perimeter of the bar. In densely reinforced members, the spaces between bars may prevent good compaction of concrete and impair bond in the finished work.

For normal weight concrete, compaction and bond are likely to be good for bars:

1   inclined at 45° to 90° to the horizontal

2   inclined at less than 45° to the horizontal and either:

- the depth of concreting does not exceed 250mm or,

- in a member of depth greater than 250mm, the bars are located in the lower half or they are at least 300mm below its top surface.

All other conditions are less favourable for bond and the normally allowable bond stress should be multiplied by 0.7.

The consequences of cracking in reinforced concrete members exposed to seawater splash are complicated by the effect of brucite accumulation which can have different effects. See 4.5.4 and 4.5.5.

Hot spots may occur in prestressed concrete in the same areas as reinforced concrete with the addition of voided ducts which may give rise to fretting and corrosion.

6.8 Summary

Loading may be deterministic or spectral.

Concrete and steel must conform to standards.

Fatigue strengths are given for concrete and steel

Analysis and assessment principles are reviewed.

Particular aspects of fatigue in bridges are highlighted.

Outline guidance is provided on looking for hot spots.

6.9 References

ARMITAGE, SIR ARTHUR (1980) Report of the Inquiry into Lorries, People and the Environment. HMSO. ISBN O 11 550536 9.

BS 5400:PART 10:1980 Steel, concrete and composite bridges. Code of practice for fatigue.

HAMBLY, E (1989) Study of tack welding of reinforcing steel. TRRL Contractor Report CR178.

PRICE, W I J, TRICKLEBANK, A H and HAMBLY, E C (1982) Fatigue considerations in the design of concrete offshore structures. IABSE Colloquium. Fatigue of steel and concrete structures. Lausanne.

PRICE, W I J, HAMBLY, E C and TRICKLEBANK, A H (1982) Review of fatigue in concrete marine structures. Concrete in the Oceans Technical Report No.12.

SEIFERT, P (1989) Fatigue loading and design for road bridges. Darmstadt-Concrete. Annual Journal on concrete and concrete structures. Vol.4. .

7 Acknowledgements

This review was prepared under contract to the Transport and Road Research Laboratory. The author wishes to thank Dr G P Tilly, Head of Structures Division, and Mr A J J Calder, Project Officer, for their encouragement and advice, TRRL Technical Illustrations Section for their careful reproduction of the Figures and Mr S Chakrabarti, Bridges Engineering Division, Department of Transport, for his helpful comments. The assistance of BE Division, BCA, BSI, CEB, CIRIA and FIP and permission to reproduce information is gratefully acknowledged.

Extracts from BS5400:Part 10:1980 are reproduced with the permission of BSI. Complete copies of the BS can be obtained by post from BSI Sales, Linford Wood, Milton Keynes, MK14 6LE; phone 0908 220022.

Appendix 1: Statistics and confidence levels

The data points from which an S-N curve is derived represent results of separate repeated loading tests with cyclic stress ranges as ordinates and the numbers of cycles to failure as abscissae. By plotting the dependent variable, log N, against the independent variable, log S, the scatter of the data points can be regarded as random variations about an underlying linear relationship: $\log N = C + m \log S$

For a particular experimental result, i:

$$\log N_i = C + m \log S_i + e_i$$

where e_i is the error component for this particular data point.

The best fit straight line is that for which $\Sigma(e_i)^2$ is a minimum.

In linear regression analysis it is assumed that the error components are normally distributed with zero mean and an unknown standard deviation.

The value of m for a set of n data points is given by:

$$m = \Sigma_{xy} / \Sigma_{xx}$$

where $\Sigma_{xy} = \Sigma \ (\log S \log N) - (1/n) \ (\Sigma \ \log S)(\Sigma \log N)$

and $\Sigma_{xx} = \Sigma \ 2.\log S - (1/n)(\Sigma \log S)^2$

The value of C can now be calculated from:

$$C = (1/n) \ \Sigma \ \log N - (m/n) \ \Sigma \log S$$

The variance of log N is obtained by dividing the residual sum of squares by (n - 2) degrees of freedom :

$$\text{Variance of } \log N = (\Sigma_{yy} - (\Sigma_{xy})^2 / \Sigma_{xx})/(n - 2)$$

where $\Sigma_{yy} = \Sigma \ 2.\log N - (1/n)(\Sigma \ \log N)^2$

The standard deviation is the square root of the variance so calculated.

A straight line parallel to the best fit line offset 2 standard deviations is commonly given as a lower bound at the 95 per cent confidence level. This is not strictly correct because the confidence interval is in fact a function of the independent variable, log S, and hyperbolic in form. It has also been assumed that the scatter has a normal distribution with the same standard deviation at all values of stress range; there is in fact less scatter at high stress than at low stress range. However the difference this makes in practical design is not significant.

Appendix 2: Fracture mechanics

A.2.1 Introduction

Reference has been made to fracture mechanics as a general approach to fatigue assessment (1.2) and in considering the fatigue performance of plain concrete (2.1). The following notes are based upon Section 6.3 of CEB Bulletin No.188 (1988) and the references given therein. In fracture mechanics there are two approaches to the study of crack initiation and propagation - the linear elastic and the non-linear.

A.2.2 Linear elastic fracture mechanics

An early approach to the problem was proposed by Griffith (1920). Assuming a perfectly elastic material up to the point of a brittle failure, the stress at the sharp tip of a crack tends to infinity as illustrated in Figure A.2.1.

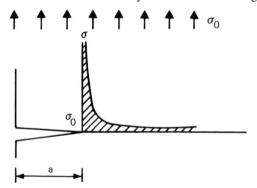

Fig. A.2.1
Stress distribution in front of crack
(Lawn and Wilshaw, 1975, CEB Bulletin No.188)

Griffith's solution to the singularity was to consider the change in the mechanical energy of the loaded structure as the crack forcing parameter. Irwin (1948,1958) extended this work by denoting the decrease in mechanical energy, U_M, per unit of crack area, A, the strain energy release rate:

$$G = -\delta\, U_M/\delta A$$

Crack initiation is associated with a critical value, G_c.

The basic parameter of fracture analysis is the stress intensity factor, K, which is considered in three possible cracking modes:

I   Opening

II   Sliding

III   Tearing

as illustrated in Figure A.2.2 due to Lawn and Wilshaw (1975).

$$K = Y(a) \; \sigma \; (\pi a)^{0.5}$$

in which Y(a) is a geometry correction factor,

a is the crack depth for a surface flaw or the half-width for a penetration flaw.

σ is the applied stress.

Expressions for K are given in standard textbooks. The critical value, K_c, for the initiation of cracking is called the fracture toughness and is determined by experiment.

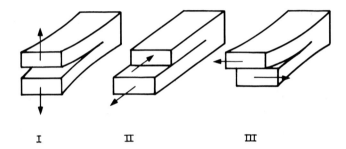

I   II   III

Fig. A.2.2
Crack extension modes
(Lawn and Wilshaw, 1975,
CEB Bulletin No.188)

The following relationships have been proved for fracture mode I:

$$G = K^2/E \qquad \text{(plane stress, thin sections)}$$

$$G = K^2(1 - (\alpha_p)^2)/E \quad \text{(plane strain, thick sections)}$$

in which E is Young's modulus and α_p is Poisson's ratio.

Crack extension per loading cycle has been expressed by Paris (1963):

$$\delta a/\delta N = C \; (\Delta K)^m$$

where $\Delta K = K_{max} - K_{min}$, the stress intensity factor range, and C and m are experimental constants from constant amplitude crack growth monitoring tests, determined by plotting log ($\delta a/\delta N$) against log (ΔK).

The Paris law fails to reflect the increased rate of crack growth as K_c is approached and Forman et al.(1967) proposed the following:

$$\delta a/\delta N = C \ (\Delta K)^m \ / \ ((1 - r)K_c - \Delta K)$$

where $r = K_{min} \ / \ K_{min}$.

For a given material the low stress range below which cracks do not propagate is known as the threshold stress intensity factor range ΔK_{th}.

The typical relationship between fatigue crack growth rate and stress intensity factor range, both in log scale, is shown in Figure A.2.3.

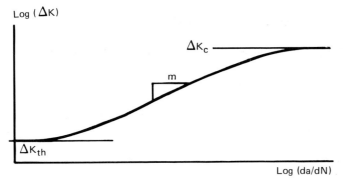

Fig. A.2.3
Fatigue crack growth rate.
(CEB Bulletin No.188)

A.2.3 Non-linear fracture mechanics

More realistic models, especially for concrete, for the stress at the crack tip were proposed by Dugdale (1960) and Barenblatt (1962) assuming a narrow non-linear zone. Rice (1968) proposed a J-integral to connect the two surfaces of the crack and developed this to follow the contour of Barenblatt's cohesive zone as indicated in Figure A.2.4.

The area below the force-separation curve, 2S, is analogous to Griffith's theory and, for limited yielding, J is analogous to G.

Finite element techniques such as those of Andersson (1973) and Hellan (1976) offer scope to model elastic and elasto-plastic behaviour.

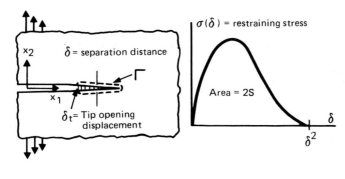

Fig. A.2.4
Cohesive force approach to
elastic brittle fracture.
(Rice,1968, CEB Bulletin
No.188)

147

A.2.4 References

ANDERSSON, H (1973) A finite element representation of stable crack growth. Journal of the Mechanics and Physics of Solids. Vol.21. pp 337-356.

BARENBLATT, G I (1962) The mathematical theory of equilibrium cracks in brittle fracture. Advances in Applied Mechanics. Vol.7 pp55-129. Academic Press, New York.

DUGDALE, D S (1960) Yielding of steel sheets containing slits. Journal of the Mechanics and Physics of Solids. Vol.8. pp100-104.

FORMAN, R G, KEARNEY, V E and ENGLE, R M (1967) Numerical analysis of crack propagation in cyclic-loaded structures. Journal of Basic Engineering. Trans. ASME pp459-464.

GRIFFITH, A A (1920) The phenomena of rupture and flow in solids. Royal Society of London. Philosophical Transactions. A Vol.221, pp163-198.

HELLAN, K (1976) Griffith-type fracture analysis for large scale yielding conditions. Engineering Fracture Mechanics. Vol.8. No.3, pp501-506.

IRWIN, G R (1947) Fracture dynamics. Fracturing of metals. A.S.M.S. October 1947 Proceedings A.S.M. Cleveland, 1948.

IRWIN, G R (1958) Fracture. Encyclopedia of Physics. Vol.6. Springer-Verlag, Berlin. pp551-590.

LAWN, B R and WILSHAW, T R (1975) Fracture of brittle solids. Cambridge University Press, pp204.

PARIS, P and ERDOGEN, F (1963) A critical analysis of crack propagation laws. Journal of Basic Engineering. Trans. ASME, Series D. Vol.85. No.4 December, pp528-534.

RICE, J R (1969) A path independent integral and the approximate analysis of strain concentration by notches and cracks.Trans. ASME. Journal of Applied Mechanics Vol.35. June, pp379-386.

Appendix 3: Variable amplitude loading

A.3.1 Introduction

Most structures are subjected to variable amplitude loading, generally of a random nature. Design or assessment loading models can be devised from site monitoring data in which case one of several counting methods is needed.

A.3.2 Spectral method

This is the simplest method and consists of counting the up-crossings of a predetermined datum as shown in Figure A.3.1.

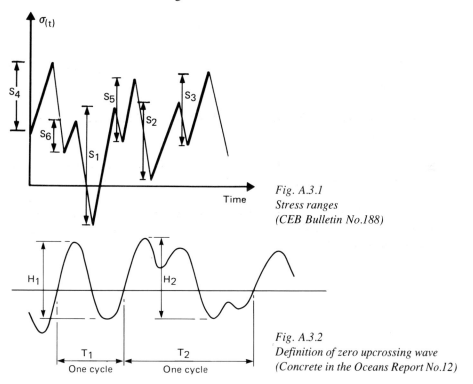

Fig. A.3.1
Stress ranges
(CEB Bulletin No.188)

Fig. A.3.2
Definition of zero upcrossing wave
(Concrete in the Oceans Report No.12)

It is the most straightforward method for collecting wave data as shown by Figure A.3.2 in which an occurrence is defined between up-crossings of zero or some other predetermined datum. Price, Hambly and Tricklebank (1989) described the system adopted to model the North Sea wave climate. Continuous records running for 12 minutes every 3 hours noted the number of up-crossings and the maximum and minimum wave height in each period. Assuming the 12 minutes represent the 3 hours and a suitable probability distribution, such as Rayleigh, the sea state is determined for each period. The probabilities of occurrence of each wave height in all of the recorded periods are then summed to give a wave height exceedance curve such as that shown in Figure A.3.3. The equation for this line is:

$$\log n = 8.3 \; (1 - H/30)$$

in which n is the number of waves of height H at the location in all directions in 50 years.

Incidences, as shown in Figure A.3.4, can then be deduced. For example, there are 119 waves with H > 22.5 m and 2873 waves with H > 17.5 m. Hence there are 2754 waves for which 17.5 m< H < 22.5 m.

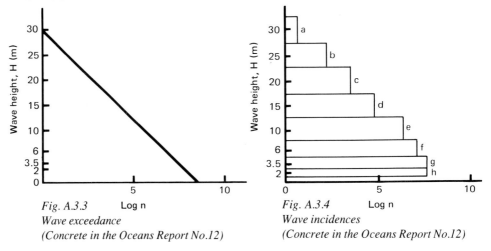

Fig. A.3.3   Log n
Wave exceedance
(Concrete in the Oceans Report No.12)

Fig. A.3.4   Log n
Wave incidences
(Concrete in the Oceans Report No.12)

A.3.3 Rainflow   method

Stress ranges are counted as differences between maximum and minimum values of each closed loop as shown on Figure A.3.5. It is attractive where interest lies in the energy dissipation described by the loops.

If it runs properly the result is generally conservative but unfortunately the rainflow is ambiguous in its normal form in a computer and presents problems in counting constant amplitude cycles.

A.3.4 Reservoir   method

This method is described in Appendix B of BS 5400: Part 10 from which Figure A.3.6 is reproduced by permission of BSI.

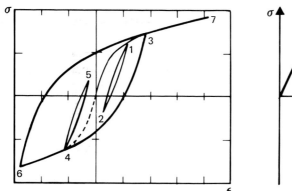
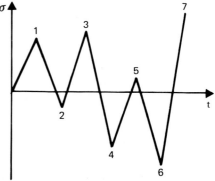

Fig. A.3.5
Rainflow method
(CEB Bulletin No.188)

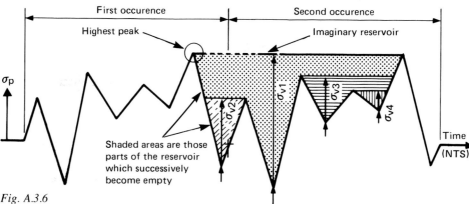

Fig. A.3.6
Reservoir method
(CEB Bulletin No.188)

This is particularly useful to transform a fairly short stress history, such as that due to the passage of a particular multi-axled vehicle, into a simple list of stress ranges. The stress history is visualised as the cross section of a reservoir which is drained successively starting with the lowest point, leaving the water that cannot escape and recording the depth drained as the stress range of each cycle. The process is repeated with the next lowest point recording the next cycle and so on until the reservoir is completely drained. The result after a number of repetitions is the same as that obtainable from the rainflow method.

A.3.5 Narrow band random loading

NBR loading is more representative of many service conditions than constant amplitude loading and is a convenient way to test steel bars at high frequencies.

The trace shown in Figure A.3.7 had a Rayleigh distribution and was produced by an

Amsler Vibrophore, an electro-magnetic resonance testing machine, running at frequencies around 150 Hz.

This was the test set up mentioned in 3.2.3.

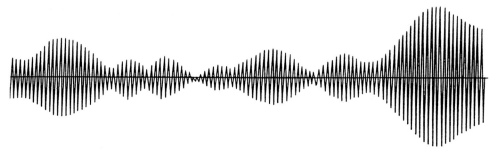

Fig. A.3.7
Typical trace of NBR loading
(Moss,SR 622)

A.3.6 TNO method

In this method, mentioned in Appendix 4 and illustrated in Figure A.3.8, each half-cycle is counted, and its period time logged, after the stress passes through the mean stress level of the total loading histogram.

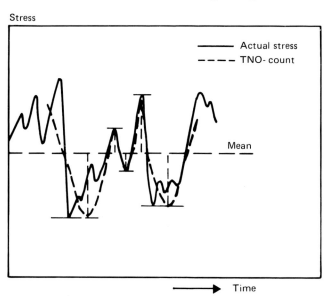

Fig. A.3.8
The TNO method
(CEB Bulletin No.188)

152

Appendix 4: Palmgren-Miner summation

A.4.1 The value of the P-M criterion

It was noted in 2.4.4 and 3.2.3 that Palmgren-Miner predictions have been compared with experimental results for concrete and steel reinforcing bars respectively. Holmen (1979), Van Leeuwen and Siemes (1979) found that the sequence effect of variable amplitude loading tends to be more damaging than the Palmgren-Miner rule predicts. For instance, 30 concrete cylinder specimens 100 mm in diameter, 250 mm high, were tested under each of the compression loading histograms shown in Figure A.4.1.

Loading histogram	Mean PM–SUM w	90% confidence interval for mean w
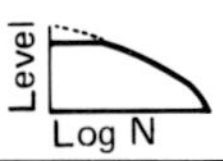 Model 2, unmodified	0.59	0.43 - 0.81
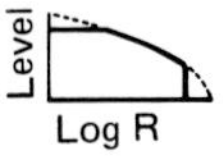 Model 2, small ampl. omitted	0.28	0.21 - 0.36
 Model 3 unmodified	0.53	0.39 - 0.72
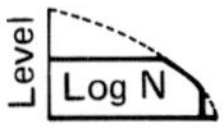 Model 3, small ampl. omitted	0.39	0.29 - 0.53
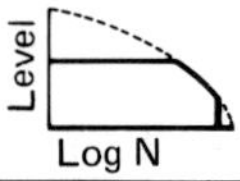 Model 3, large ampl. truncated	0.30	0.22 - 0.40
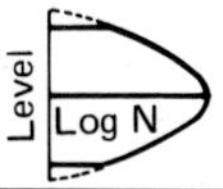 Model 1, unmodified	0.84	0.64 - 1.11
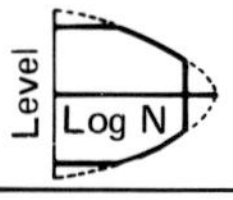 Model 1, small ampl. omitted	0.75	0.52 - 1.06

Fig. A.4.1
P-M sums for compression loading histograms
(Holmen, 1979, CEB Bulletin No.188)

153

Two basic histograms had constant $\sigma_{min} = 0.05\ f_{cm}$ and $\sigma_{rm} = 0.50\ f_{cm}$ respectively and these were modified by omitting small amplitudes or truncating large ones. All tests were run at 5 Hz.

Small amplitude cycles tend to improve fatigue performance and removing them is detrimental. Values of ω were related to the cycle ratio, σ_{min}/σ_{ck} in which σ_{ck}, the characteristic stress level, is defined as the mean stress, σ_{rm}, plus the RMS value of the load signal. Mean values are plotted logarithmically in Figure A.4.2.

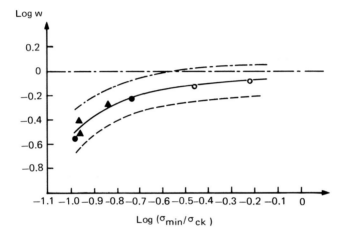

Fig. A.4.2
P-M number, , for
compression loading
histograms
(Holmen, 1979, CEB Bulletin
No.188)

A large number of small amplitude cycles tends to increase the cycle ratio and the P-M number,ω , tends to a value of 1.

Unfortunately this relationship cannot be applied generally. In particular, it is not necessarily valid for multi-stage constant amplitudes or for other types of random loading or for other frequencies.

Cornelissen and Siemes (1985) reported random compression loading tests at frequencies between 0.16 and 6 Hz. They used the TNO counting method described in Appendix 3 and their computation took account of the frequency of each half-cycle. They found a mean value for ω of 0.87 with a standard deviation of 0.26.

In practice, Palmgren-Miner summations for different details tend to range very much more widely than this. Van Leeuwen and Siemes (1979) showed that, for tests on plain concrete, the scatter of ω values has a log-normal distribution with a mean less than 1. Waagard (1981) suggested values between 0.2 and 0.5; Det norske Veritas stipulate a value of 0.2 with a life of more than 20 years. The nature of the basic S-N relationship produces large changes in N, sometimes orders of magnitude, from quite small changes in S so that, although the Palmgren-Miner Rule is by no means precise, there is seldom any difficulty in deciding whether or not a feature is acceptable.

Moss (1980) compared the results of NBR loading tests on 16 mm continuous and butt welded reinforcing bars with performance curves calculated from the Palmgren-Miner

Rule using a critical value of 1. His results are shown in Figures A.4.3 and A.4.4. See also 3.2.3 and A.3.5.

Application of the Rule is illustrated by two examples.

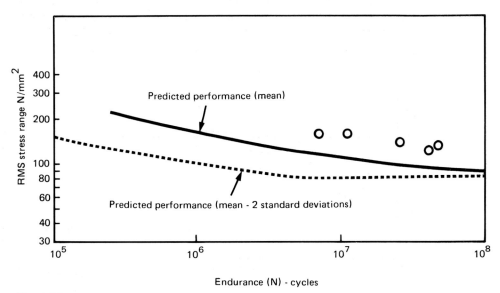

Fig. A.4.3
Fatigue of 16 mm continuous bar
(Moss, TRRL Supplementary Report 622)

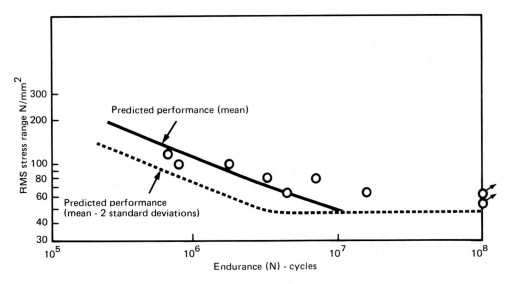

Fig. A.4.4
Fatigue of 16 mm butt welded bar
(Moss, TRRL Supplementary Report 622)

A.4.2 Transverse slab of bridge deck

This example is an extension of work by Hambly (1989) in a study for TRRL to develop fatigue rules for unwelded reinforcing bars.

A 200 mm thick deck slab spans 3 m between longitudinal beams. The ultimate limit state is governed by HB wheel loads and, after satisfying criteria for the serviceability limit state, the design resulted in 16 mm high yield bars at 150 mm centres with 45 mm cover. The fatigue check is concerned with a transverse bar at midspan between beams.

Assuming the centre of the traffic lane to be 600 mm from a support beam and using charts due to Pucher (1964), it was found that the stress in the bar is 0.43 N/mm² per kN of axle load. Applying the full vehicle spectrum given in Table 11 of BS 5400: Part 10, it was found that most of the fatigue damage is due to heavy 4-axle articulated vehicles (designated 4A-H in Table 11) and lesser ones. The total damage in 120 years was calculated assuming Class R1 with the σ_r-N relationship:

$$N (\sigma_r)^9 = 0.75 \times 10^{27}$$

for N up to 10 million cycles and changing the exponent of the σ_r-N from 9 to 11 for longer endurances. The summation came to 2.5×10^{-6} which showed that there is no fatigue risk in this case.

The calculation was repeated using an arbitrary major corrosion relationship:

$$N (\sigma_r)^9 = 0.21 \times 10^{23}$$

The summation came to 0.91 which showed that the design would be close to the limit for the design life of 120 years if major corrosion occurred.

The following calculation tests the same design with the criteria proposed in the CEB Model Code for straight 16 mm bars but increasing the stresses and applying a reduction factor of 1.7 to allow for major corrosion.

The relationship is:

$$N (\sigma_r)^9 = 1.30 \times 10^{25} \text{ modified where N exceeds 10 million.}$$

$$\text{or log } N = 25.11 - 9 \log \sigma_r \text{ for log } N \leq 7$$

$$\text{or log } N = 29.14 - 11 \log \sigma_r \text{ for log } N > 7$$

Vehicle	Axle kN	σ_r N/mm^2	Endurance N	Millions of passes n	Damage n/N
4A-H	100	57	6.7×10^9	21.6	0.0032
	90	52	1.8×10^{10}	43.2	0.0023
4A-M	85	48	4.4×10^{10}	21.6	0.0005
4R-H	90	52	1.8×10^{10}	3.6	0.0002
3A-H	85	48	4.4×10^{10}	7.2	0.0002
3R-H	90	52	1.8×10^{10}	3.6	0.0002
2R-H	85	48	4.4×10^{10}	40.8	0.0009
			This total damage is clearly not critical		0.0075

For a sample calculation with an assessment of present fatigue damage, assume that the slab reinforcement is lapped at midspan with medium bends at the joggles and it has severe corrosion.

The fatigue strength at 10 million cycles, for these conditions, is 105 / 1.7 = 62 N/mm².

Vehicle	σ_r N/mm^2	N millions	n millions	n/N damage
4A-H	57	25.2	21.6	0.86
	52	69.2	43.2	0.62
4A-M	48	166.8	21.6	0.13
4R-H	52	69.2	3.6	0.05
3A-H	48	166.8	7.2	0.04
3R-H	52	69.2	3.6	0.05
2R-H	48	166.8	40.8	0.24
			Total	1.99

As the number of vehicle passes was calculated for a service life of 120 years, the above summation suggests a life of only about 60 years.

If the bridge was constructed in 1935 and pitting-corrosion started in 1950, the proposals give the following factors for the loss of section and the loading for each decade.

Decade	Percentage loss of section	Stress factor	Loading spectrum factor
1950-59	6.25	1.07	0.25
1960-69	12.5	1.14	0.75
1970-79	18.75	1.23	1.00
1980-89	25	1.33	1.00

Hence the damage can be calculated for each decade.

Vehicle	σ_r	N	n	n/N	σ_r	N	n	n/N
	1950-59				1960-69			
4A-H	46	266	1.8	0.007	49	133	1.8	0.014
	42	725	3.6	0.005	45	340	3.6	0.011
4A-M	39	1639	1.8	0.001	41	946	1.8	0.002
3A-H	39	1639	0.6	-	41	946	0.6	-
2R-H	39	1639	3.4	0.002	41	946	3.4	0.004
			Total	0.015			Total	0.031

Vehicle	σ_r	N	n	n/N	σ_r	N	n	n/N
	1970-79				1980-89			
4A-H	53	56	1.8	0.032	57	25	1.8	0.071
	48	167	3.6	0.022	52	69	3.6	0.052
4A-M	44	435	1.8	0.004	48	167	1.8	0.011
3A-H	44	435	0.6	0.001	48	167	0.6	0.004
2R-H	44	435	3.4	0.008	48	167	3.4	0.020
			Total	0.067			Total	0.158

The total damage over the four decades comes to 0.271 leaving a future damage fraction of 0.729. Assuming that further loss of section will be prevented by waterproofing or cathodic protection, the remaining life will be spent at the same rate as the last decade. This suggests that the detail has a useful further life of some 10 x 0.729/0.158 = 46 years.

As a completely different scenario, suppose there is no loss of section but that a fixture had been welded to several of these bars or that the welder caused accidental damage. The appropriate fatigue strength for this situation is 100 N/mm^2 at 2 million cycles with (m + 2) = 5.

The relationship is log N = 16.30 - 5 log σ_r

Vehicle	Axle kN	σ_r N/mm^2	Millions N	Millions of passes n	Damage n/N
4A-H	100	43	136	21.6	0.16
	90	39	222	43.2	0.19
4A-M	85	36	331	21.6	0.06
3A-H	85	36	331	7.2	0.02
2R-H	85	36	331	40.8	0.12
				Others	0.05
				Total	0.60

This could be interpreted as a fatigue life of about 200 years.

A.4.3 Post-tensioned bridge beam

A 26 m span in a multi-span flyover carries a dual 3-lane carriageway trunk road. The superstructure comprises contiguous precast post-tensioned concrete I-beams with post-tensioned diaphragms and an in situ concrete deck. Assuming that there are voids in the ducts, the fatigue check is concerned with fretting of a severely corroded prestressing tendon in an outer beam. Stresses in the tendon due to the spectrum of vehicles given in BS5400 were calculated from the known distributed effect of HA loading in the outer lane.

The fatigue strength at 1 million cycles is $50/1.7 = 29$ N/mm^2 and $m = 5$.

The relationships are $\log N = 13.31 - 5 \log \sigma_r$ for $\sigma_r < 29$ N/mm^2 or $\log N = 11.85 - 4 \log \sigma_r$ for $\sigma_r > 29$ N/mm^2

Vehicle	Total kN	σ_r N/mm^2	Millions N	Millions of passes n	Damage n/N
18GT-H	3680	37	0.38	0.0036	0.0095
M	1520	15	27	0.0108	0.0004
9TT-H	1610	33	0.6	0.0036	0.0060
7GT-H	1310	19	8.3	0.0054	0.0006
5A-M	360	8	626	2.61	0.0042
L	250	5	6563	2.70	0.0004
4A-H	335	8	626	16.2	0.0259
M	260	5	6563	16.2	0.0025
4R-H	280	7	1220	2.7	0.0021
M	240	5	6563	2.7	0.0004
3A-H	215	5	6563	5.4	0.0008
3R-H	240	6	2637	2.7	0.0010
M	195	5	6563	2.7	0.0004
2R-H	135	3	84400	30.6	0.0004
				Total	0.0346

This suggests a fatigue life in excess of 120 years whilst the integrity of the concrete and prestressing steel areas assumed in design remains unimpaired. If corrosion resulted in the failure of one or more wires or tendons, then loss of prestress, cracking and deflection would become evident. Routine inspections would pick up such signs long before the collapse state and the complex analysis of low-cycle fatigue which might ultimately contribute to failure is therefore academic and beyond the scope of this work.

A.4.4 References

BS 5400:PART 10:1980 Steel, concrete and composite bridges. Code of practice for fatigue.

CORNELISSEN, H A W and SIEMES, A J M (1985) Plain concrete under sustained tensile or tensile and compressive fatigue loading. Proc. BOSS Conference. Elsevier Science Publishers B.V. Amsterdam. pp487-498.

HAMBLY, E (1989) Study of tack welding of reinforcing steel. TRRL Contractor Report CR178.

HOLMEN, J O (1979) Fatigue of concrete by constant and variable amplitude loading. Bulletin No.79-1, Division of Concrete Structures, NTH,Trondheim.

MOSS, D S (1980) Axial fatigue of high-yield reinforcing bars in air. TRRL Report SR622.

PUCHER, A (1964) Influence surfaces of elastic plates. Springer Verlag. Wien and New York.

VAN LEEUWEN, J and SIEMES, A J M (1979) Miner's Rule with respect to concrete. 2nd International Conference on Behaviour of Offshore Structures.

WAAGARD, K (1981) Fatigue strength evaluation of offshore concrete structures. ACI Convention on Fatigue, Dallas.

Appendix 5: Some aspects of calculating stresses in reinforced and prestressed concrete members under fatigue loading

Appendix A from CEB Bulletin D'Information No 188, by permission of CEB

A.5.1 Scope

At the beginning of life the relationship between loading and stress in a fatigue loaded member does not differ from any other loaded member. The stresses at this time can be calculated using the same models and constitutive laws as for the other loads. However, during service life stresses can change due to time - dependent changes in the behaviour of the material (e.g. creep, loss of bond).

In the following, proposals for stress calculation are made which take this time-dependent behaviour into account. For prestressed members the effect of stress redistribution between reinforcing steel and prestressing steel is also considered.

The background for these proposals is only briefly described, more information can be taken from the references.

A.5.2 Stresses in reinforced concrete members

In general the stresses are calculated by setting compatibility and equilibrium between internal and external forces using the same constitutive laws as for usual design situations.

161

A.5.2.1 Members with a small amount of tensile reinforcement

In such members the concrete in the bending compression zone behaves in a linear manner (Figure A.5.1) and the stresses in the tensile reinforcement and stirrups (rectangular cross section) can be calculated as follows:

$$\text{lever arm } z = d - x/3 \tag{1}$$

$$\text{where } x = (a_e A_s/b) \cdot (((1+ (2bd/a_e A_s))^{0.5}-1) \tag{2}$$

with the modular ratio $\alpha_e = E_s/E_c$

and E_s = modulus of elasticity of steel

E_c = modulus of elasticity of concrete

The stress in the tensile reinforcement is given by

$$\sigma_s = (I/A_s) \cdot ((M/z) + (Q/2)) \tag{3}$$

and the stress in the stirrups by

$$\sigma_{sv} = Q/a_{sv} \cdot z \tag{4}$$

where M is bending Moment

and Q is shear force

and a_{sv} is cross section of stirrups/unit of length.

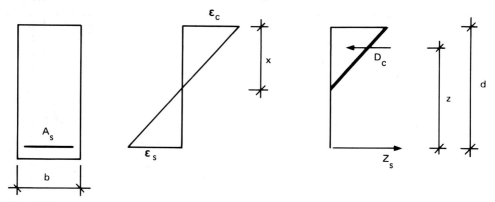

Fig. A.5.1
Strain and stress in lightly reinforced members
(CEB Bulletin No.188)

The effect of creep in the bending compression zone due to dead load and perhaps a part of the fatigue load can be considered with a reduced modulus of elasticity E_c for the concrete. Investigations of various researchers have shown that the modulus of elasticity for concrete decreases after a relatively small number of load cycles (10 % of life) to a value of about 0,7 - 0,8 . $E_{c, t = 0}$. Subsequently this value remains almost constant up to 90% of service life and then rapidly decreases. This effect is taken in account assuming $\alpha_e = 10$.

A.5.2.2 Members with a large amount of tensile reinforcement

The stresses have to be calculated using the constitutive laws for concrete and steel illustrated in Figure A.5.2.

The stress is calculated by taking into account equilibrium between internal and external forces and compatibility in strains between concrete and steel (see Figure A.5.3).

The equivalent concrete stress σ_c is required for the fatigue check.

The stresses in the tensile reinforcement and in the stirrups can be calculated using equ. (3) and (4), whereas the lever arm, z, appropriate to the beginning of service life, has to be calculated according to Figure A.5.3.

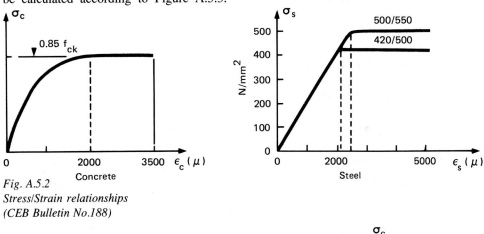

Fig. A.5.2
Stress/Strain relationships
(CEB Bulletin No.188)

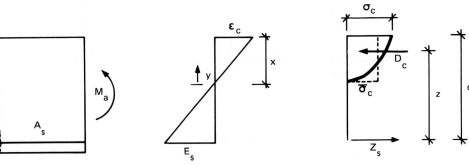

Fig. A.5.3
Strain and stress in heavily reinforced member
(CEB Bulletin No.188)

A.5.3 Prestressed concrete members

The formation of cracks in prestressed concrete members depends mainly on the degree of prestressing. Because there is a direct relationship between stresses and crack formation, the following two cases must be considered:

1   partially prestressed members

2   almost fully prestressed members

In the first case the maximum concrete tensile stress under design load conditions exceeds the tensile strength of concrete. In the second case the concrete tensile stress is small.

For partially prestressed members calculation of stresses has to be done assuming a final crack pattern, whereas in the other case the calculation is based on a single crack formation.

A.5.3.1 Partially prestressed members

As the first step the whole tensile force Z at the centre of gravity of the total reinforcement (reinforcing steel + prestressing steel) has to be calculated neglecting tension stiffening (see Figure A.5.4).

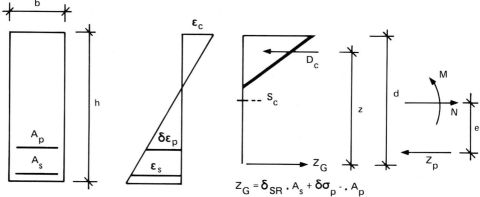

$$Z_G = \delta_{SR} \cdot A_s + \delta\sigma_p \cdot A_p$$

Fig. A.5.4
Strain and stress in partially prestressed member
(CEB Bulletin No.188)

164

For the second step the stress in the reinforcing steel σ_s and the stress increase in the prestressing steel $\zeta\sigma_p$ can be calculated as follows:

$$\sigma_s = \frac{Z_s}{A_s + A_p} + \frac{0.3 \cdot f_{ct} \cdot A_p}{A_s + \zeta_1 \cdot A_p} \cdot \frac{1 - \zeta_1}{A_s + A_p} \cdot A_{b,eff} \quad (5)$$

$$\delta\sigma_p = \frac{Z_s}{A_s + A_p} + \frac{0.3 \cdot f_{ct} \cdot A_g}{A_s + \zeta_1 \cdot A_p} \cdot \frac{\zeta_1 - 1}{A_s + A_p} \cdot A_{b,eff} \quad (6)$$

with f_{ct} : = tensile strength of concrete

$\zeta_1 = \zeta \cdot (\varnothing / \varnothing_p)$

$A_{b,eff} = 3 \cdot b \, (h-d)$

$\varnothing_s$ = diameter of reinforcing steel

$\varnothing_p$ = diameter of prestressing steel

(for bundles an equivalent diameter has to be chosen:

1.6 $(A_v)^{0.5}$ with A_v = cross section area of the bundle)

for post tensioned members

$\zeta = 0{,}2$ for smooth prestressing stee

$\zeta = 0{,}4$ for strands

$\zeta = 0{,}6$ for ribbed prestressing steels

for pre tensioned members

$\zeta = 0.6$ for strands

$\zeta = 0.8$ for ribbed prestressing steel

A.5.3.2 Almost fully prestressed concrete members

In these cases only single cracks would be expected and the stiffness of the tensile zone is much greater than in partially prestressed members. This must be considered as far as the calculation of stresses is concerned.

The tensile force is: $Z = s_s \cdot A_s + ds_p \cdot A_p$ (7)

with $ds_p/s_s = (z \cdot \varnothing_s / \varnothing_p)^{0.5}$ (8)

The force Z can be calculated using the total force Z^I of the tensile zone in the uncracked state (I), due to the external loads and the prestressing force.

$Z = 0.9 \cdot Z^I$ (9)

A.5.4 References

CORNELISSEN, H.A.W. (1987) Fatigue performance of concrete. Contribution to the CEB General Task Group 15 "Fatigue of Concrete Structures".

FREY, R.P. (1985) Ermüdung von Stahlbetonbalken unter Biegung und Querkraft, Lausanne.

HASHEM, M. (1986) Betriebsfestigkeitsnachweis von biegebeanspruchten Stahlbeton-bauteilen. Dissertation Darmstadt.

JANOVIC, L and KUPFER, H.: Teilweise Vorspannung - Plattenversuche.DafStb Heft 351

KÖNIG G., FEHLING, E., (1987) u.a.: Mindestbewehrung und Rißbreitenbeschränkung im Spannbetonbau, Institut für Massivbau der TH Darmstadt, Forschungsbericht.

TROST, H., CORDES, H., THORMÄLEN, H and HAGEN, H.: Teilweise Vorspannung - Verbundfestigkeit von Spann-gliedern und ihre Bedeutung für Rißbildung und Riß - breitenbeschrankung. DafStb Heft 310.

REHM, G., Eligenhausen, R.: Verbundverhalten von gerippten Betonstahlen mit kurzer Einbettungslänge bei nicht ruhender Belastung Untersuchungsbericht Nr. 75/17 des Lehrstuhls für Werkstoffe im Bauwesen an der Universität Stuttgart.

Printed in the United Kingdom for HMSO.
Dd.294403, 4/91, C10, 3390/3, 5673, 145394.